AF572071

GAGOSIAN GALLERY

Elyn Zimmerman New Drawings

with essays by Amy Hempel and Pepe Karmel

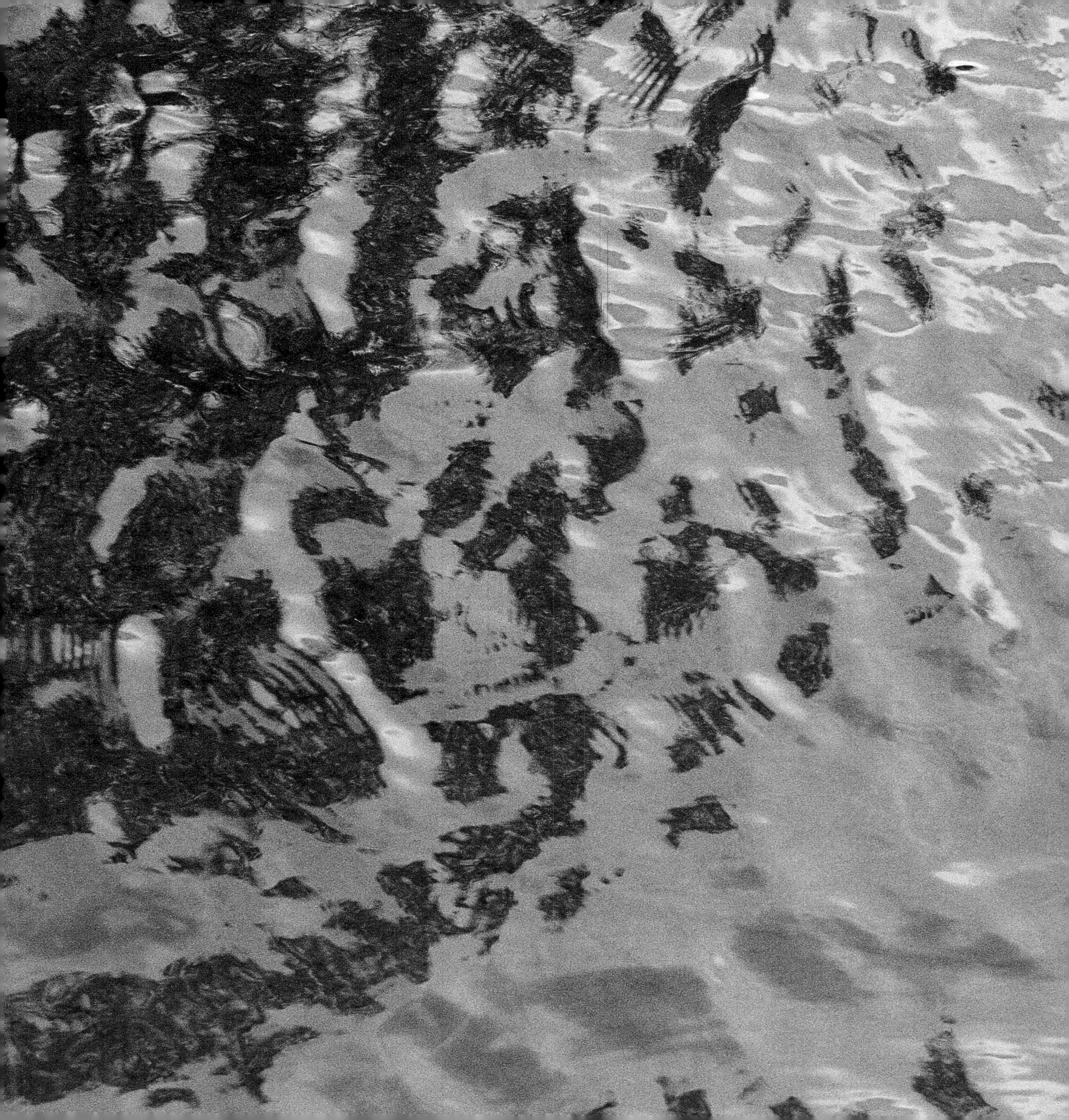

ELYN ZIMMERMAN'S WATERY PRISMATICS

by Amy Hempel

In an old mill town in northern Vermont, the Gihon River flows beneath a bridge that connects the mill – now an artists' colony—to the main street of town. In the fall of 2000, Elyn Zimmerman was Visiting Artist-in-Residence. I first saw her leaning over the bridge, pointing a camera at the shallow water that passes over stones below.

She had borrowed the camera, it turned out, after she arrived and saw that her studio overlooked the river. She acquired something else there; after a day of making studio visits to young artists, she went to the art supply store, needing something to do with her hands.

"All they had that I wanted to invest in was paper and ink," Zimmerman said. "And I thought: why not? Cheap paper, cheap brushes, cheap ink—let's have some fun, no one's going to see this."

The resulting photographs and ink drawings are "watery prismatics," to borrow a phrase from a Mark Doty poem. And although a prism refracts light into a spectrum of *colors*, Zimmerman's prismatics are the shadow shades of water and stone. ("Shadow is the queen of colors," declared Saint Augustine).

It is a body of work, a liquid mother lode, that calls up limitless associations. A sometime scuba diver, Zimmerman notes that water moves differently down deep than it does at the surface. And even in deep water, it is the sight of light from above—on coral walls, or in currents—that gets her attention.

Water Study, gelatin silver print, 2000

These photos and drawings vividly evoked a favorite activity of my Wasted Youth; in summer, when it rained, I would sink myself near the shoreline of a lake and look up to see where rain pebbled the surface. It was the way I felt *elemental.* Zimmerman's work engenders this response, is inclusive in this way too. And just as we are not good or bad, but good *and* bad, her surfaces—corrugated and kaleidoscopic, skeletal and striated—are both broken *and* continuous, agitated *and* becalmed, fractured and reassembled.

"It's not that I'm doing these because I'm so in love with *water*," the artist said. "I'm in love with light and surface and texture and the *interface."* Or, to put it another way: not water, but wave, "which is not water... but a force which water welcomes and displays" (William Matthews).

"And," allowed Zimmerman, laughing, "because it works with all the *other* black and white things I've done. It's part of a vocabulary. I bought colored inks when I got back from Vermont, and they looked awful, tawdry. I'm not color-phobic, but..."

Precedent for Zimmerman's affinity for black and white includes her "Equivalent Abstractions"—identical photographs and graphite drawings of her studio interior in Los Angeles, made in 1974 (pages 8-9). The way light broke through a window upon the wall and floor, evidence of the ways in which something known can become emblematic of what is beyond our reckoning.

Just before Zimmerman went to Vermont, she installed a large stone sculpture on Long Island, in Southampton (page 61). She turned it on and saw water flow around stone in the contained pool she had designed (page 63). The light off the ocean and the light on the water in the pool preconfigured what she would find the following week in the river. And in Vermont, "I didn't want to render something in nature," she said. "I was just looking in the water and thinking about how it moved when it hit stone, since that's what I work with a lot, and liking the interference patterns at different times of the day."

The ink drawings, gestural and immediate, are "a *trace* of a thought or action," she said.

And how did she know when she "had" something?

"When I feel I 'get' something, it's because some level of noise in my life has been turned off. When I first moved to New York, a line from T.S. Eliot was running through my mind: 'Distracted from distraction by distraction.' I felt I couldn't focus; I did all these black and white photographs of buildings where the buildings were dissolving—either in fog, or I'd move the camera slightly so they'd blur—I was trying to de-materialize these things." (pages 58-59).

I think of the poets when I see these *new* photos and drawings: "The way to move upon water/Is to work lying down, as in love"—James Dickey (or perhaps leaning over, from above!). "One drop of water entirely awake"—Anne Carson. "The surface, now overrun with the high travel of clouds"—Billy Collins. Maybe even Rumi: "Not only the thirsty seek the water/the water as well seeks the thirsty."

And what of the "message"? Francine du Plessix Gray, asked about a *writer's* obligation to take a political stance in her work, answered that she felt a writer's only obligation was to write well. Zimmerman, whose public art credentials include "Marabar" at the National Geographic Society in Washington, "Terrain" at O'Hare International Center in Chicago, and the World Trade Center Memorial in New York City, said, "I think the *public* art I do addresses social issues because you're making a *place*—you meet with community boards, and you deal with how people *use* the space. You're deep in politics—not *art world* politics, but *street* politics: who's paying the bills, who's in power, etc.

"It's not fashionable in the art world to deal with things that don't have a social or political or psychological message. But I think there is also something to be said for art that somehow transcends contemporary issues and has a deeper resonance,

Equivalent Abstraction I, 1974
14 photographs each 14½″ x 19½″ and 14 graphite drawings each 14½″ x 19½″
Collection: Whitney Museum of American Art

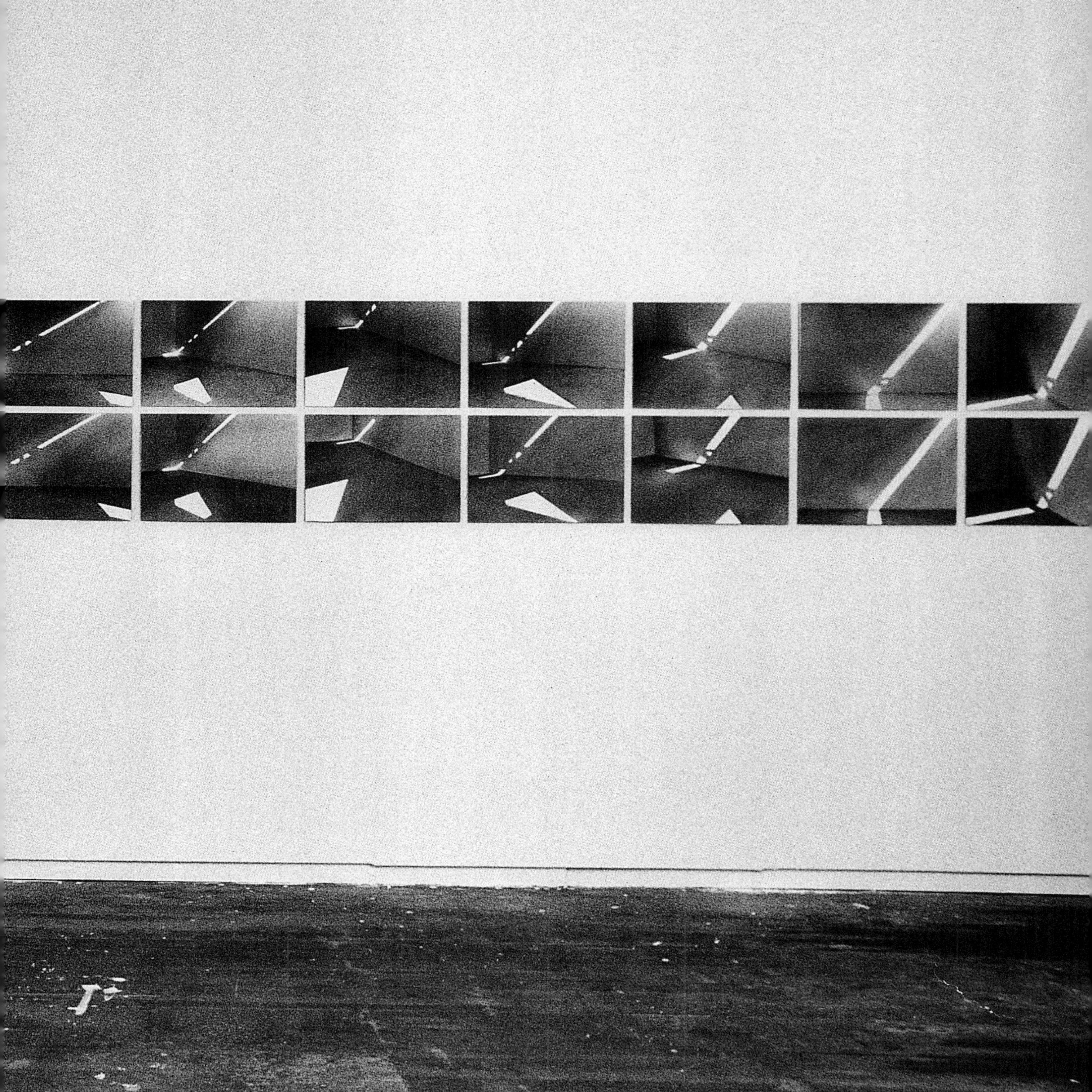

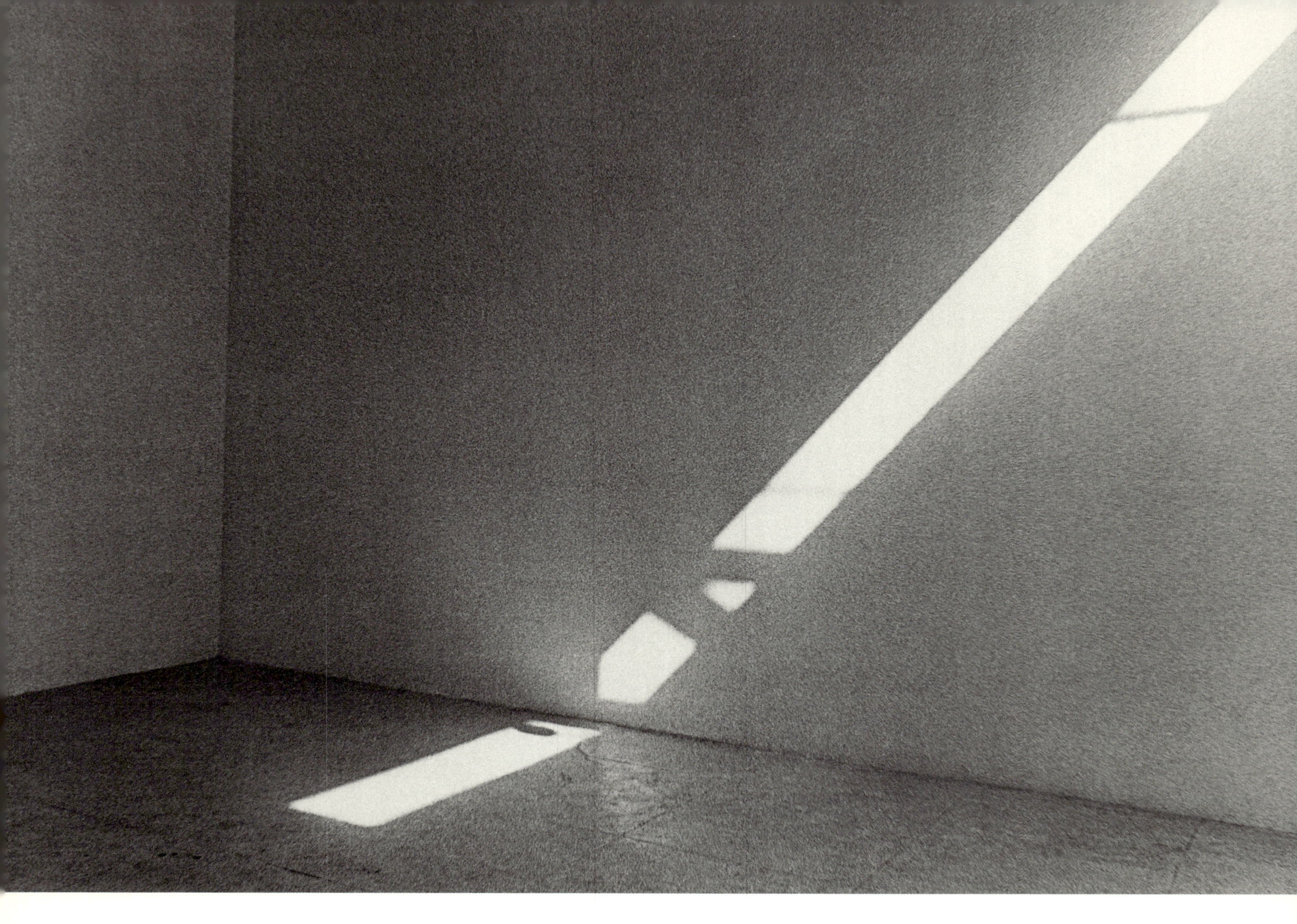

Equivalent Abstraction I, 1974
Detail, photograph

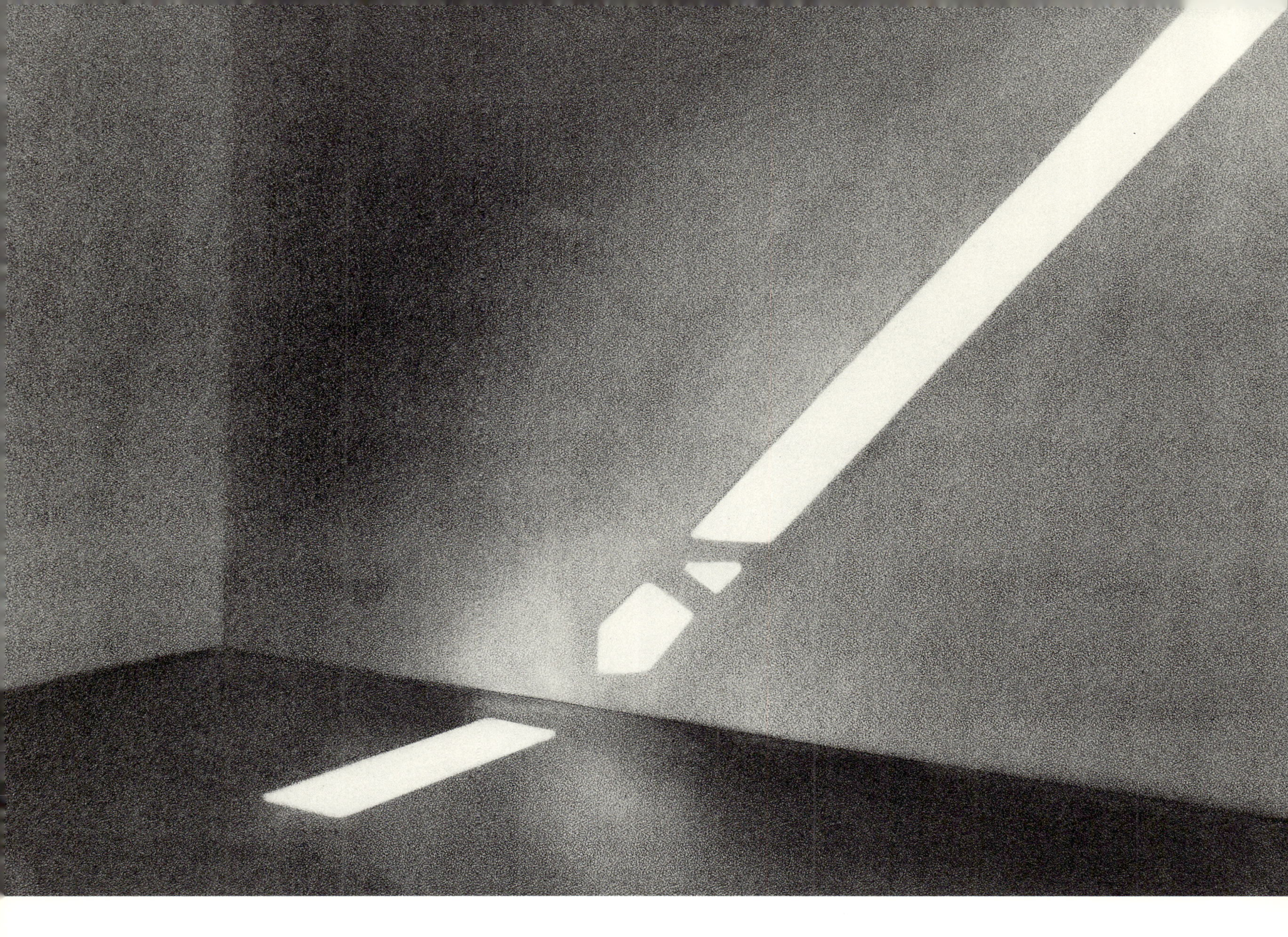

Equivalent Abstraction I, 1974
Detail, graphite drawing

that reflects parts of themselves that people are too busy to be in touch with. If you can sometimes nail that, you've done a lot." Do that, Gordon Lish has said, and people will look "to find out how you solved being alive."

An old friend and I used to think that the solutions to our problems could be had, would be revealed, by floating ourselves in water face down, eyes open to the sandy floor, contemplative, trying to interpret the patterns as a fortune teller might read tea leaves. Zimmerman, it turns out, has a kind of synchronous notion:

"You know those 8-balls with the dark liquid in them? You turn it over and there's a window with the answer to your question floating in it? I always think of the mind like that," she said, "as if the mental ball in my mind has been turned over and something has come up to the window, and then I can read it."

The thing is, you have to keep turning it and turning it if you want to get the *right* answer. And that is what Zimmerman does, turning drawing after drawing, each one putting the question: Is this the most effective point of entry?

The answer each time is: Yes.

Following pages:
Water Study, gelatin silver print, 2000

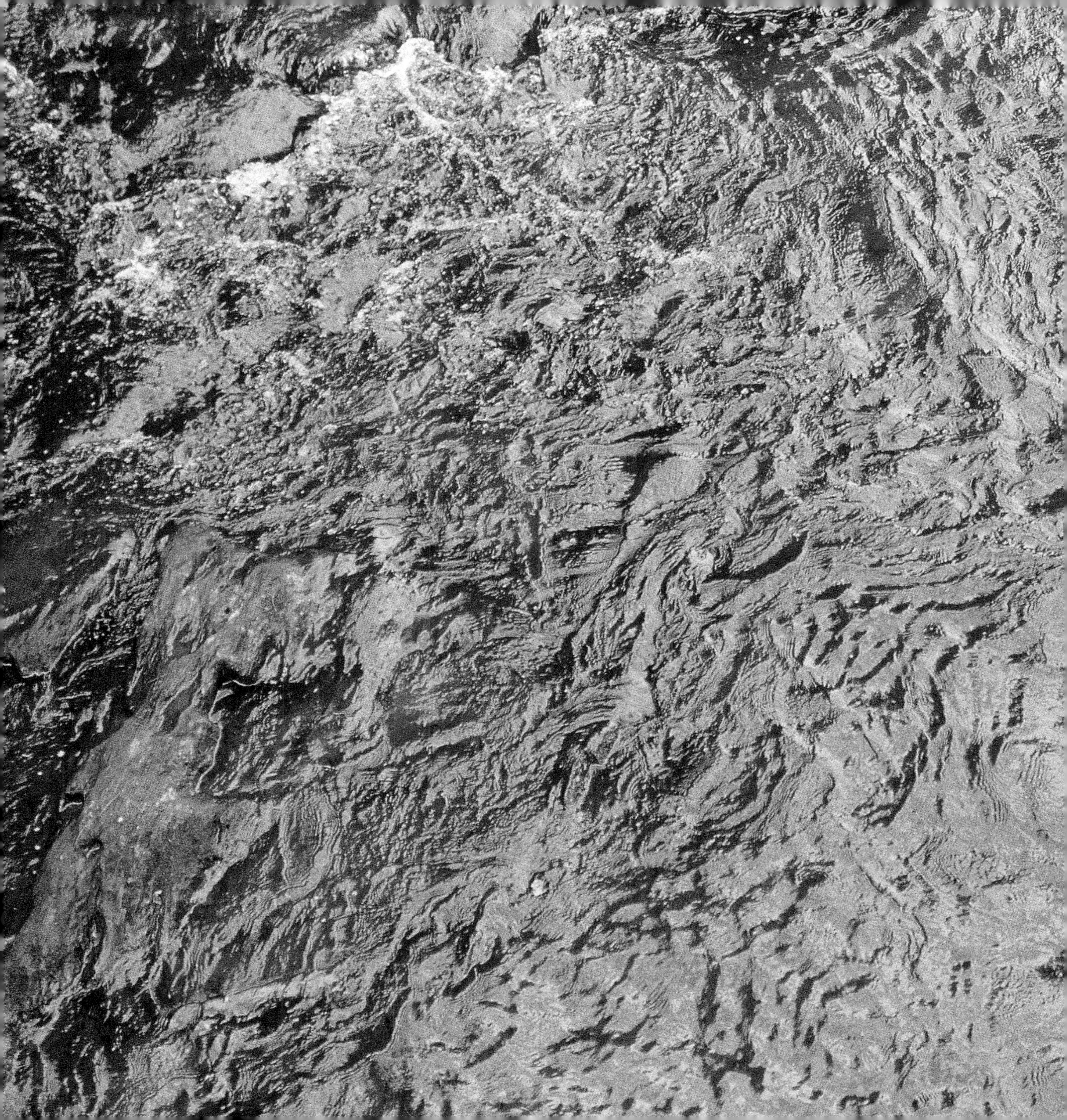

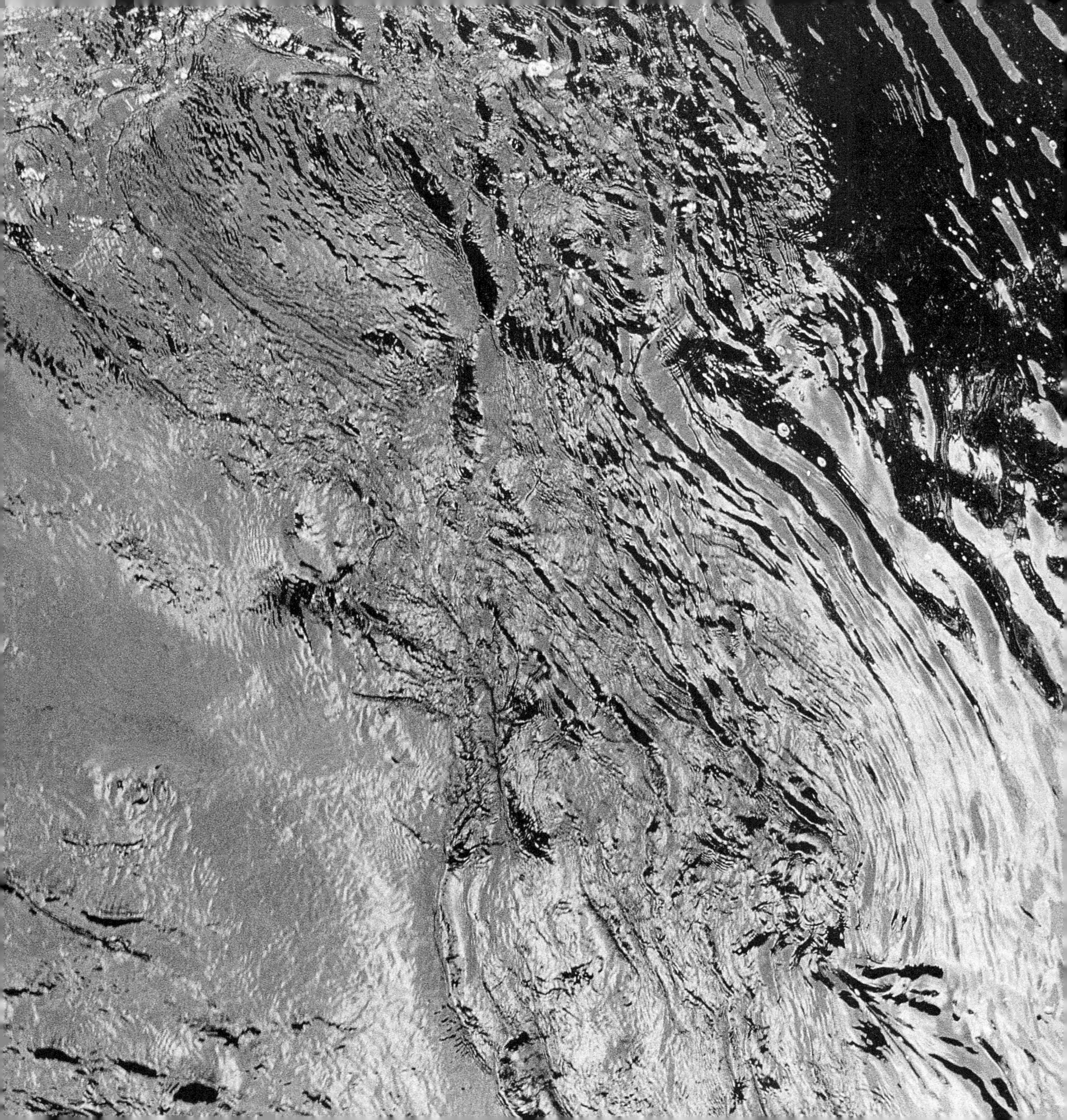

PLATES

PLATE I

Untitled 5, 2000–2001

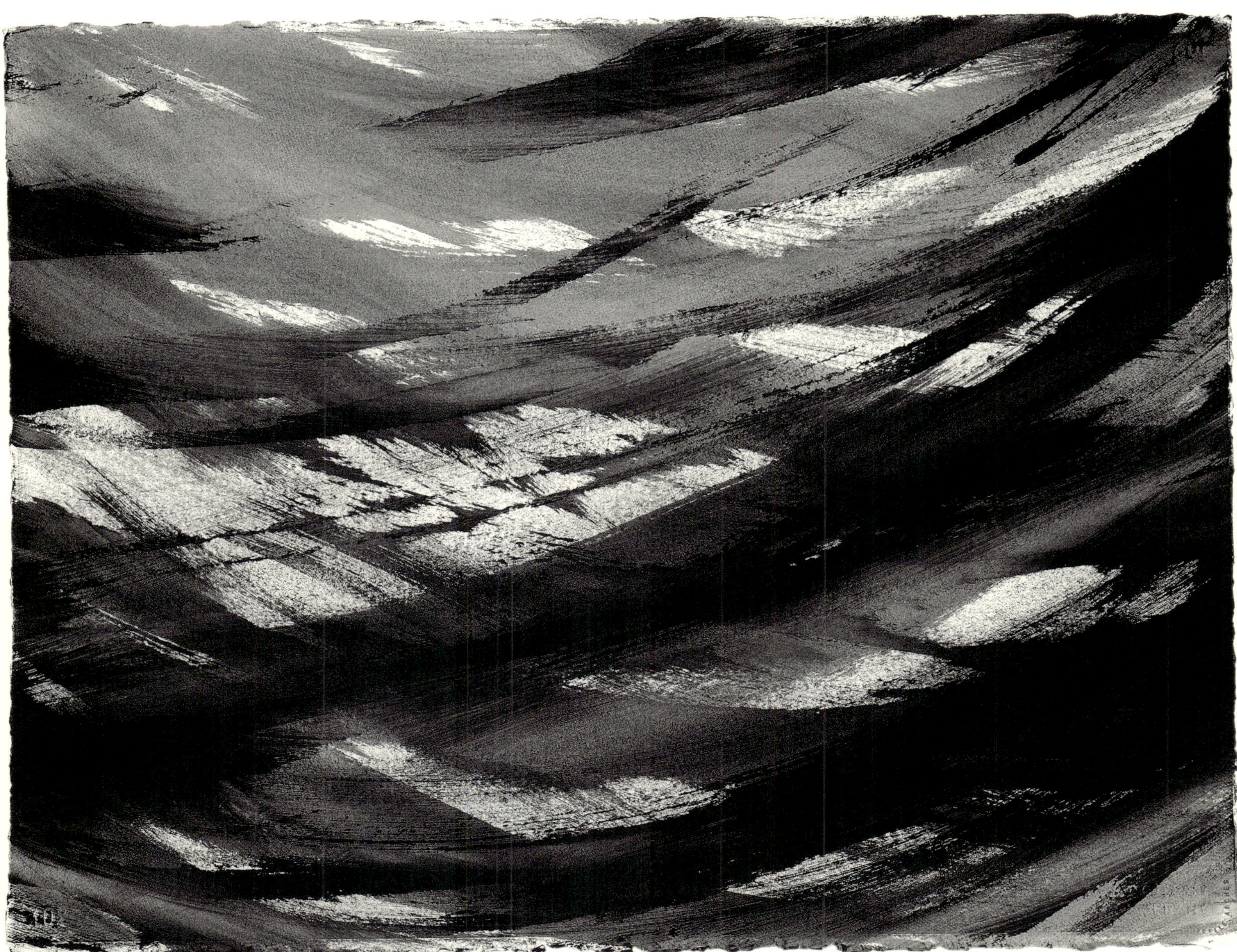

18

PLATE II

Untitled 7, 2001

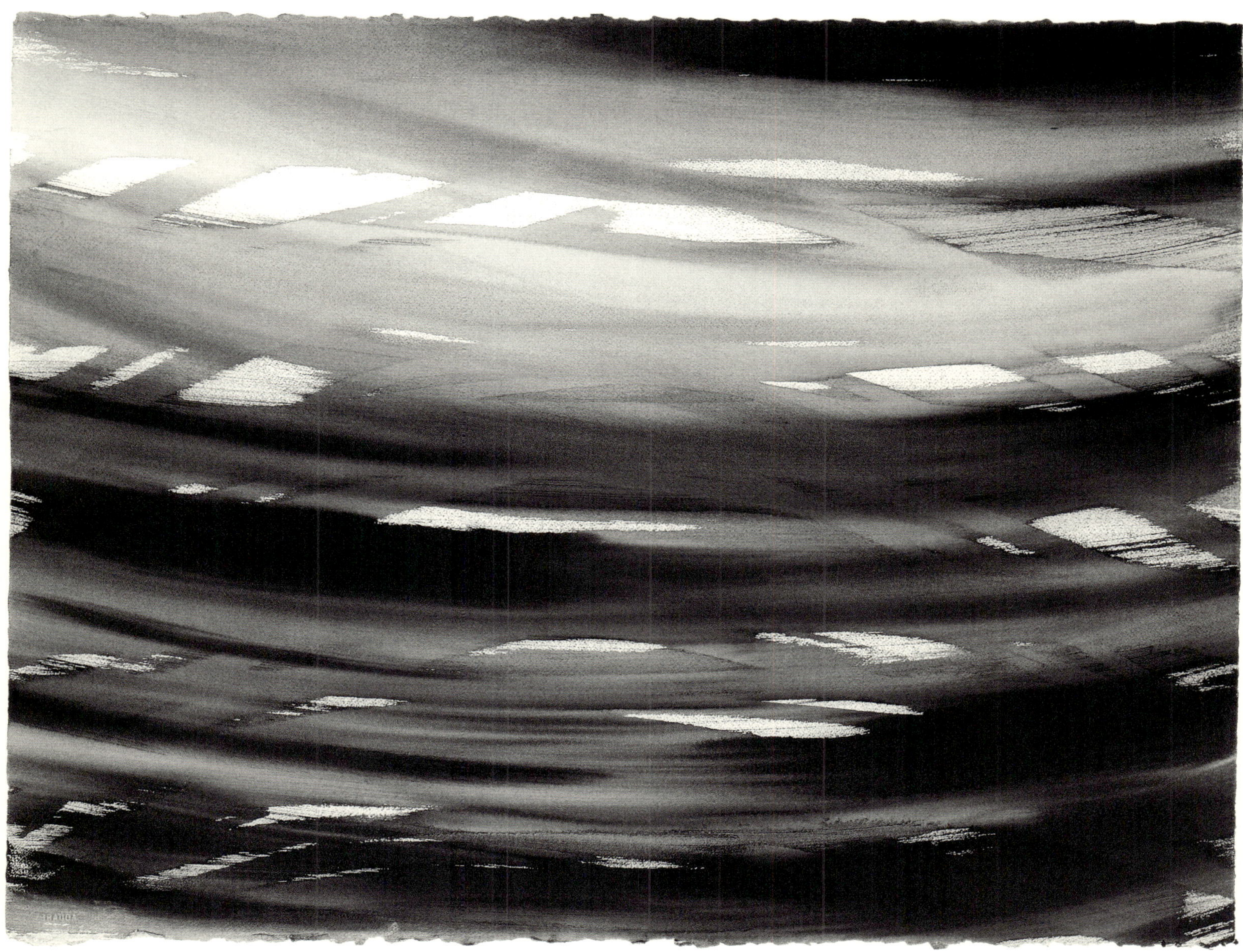

PLATE III

Untitled 13, 2001

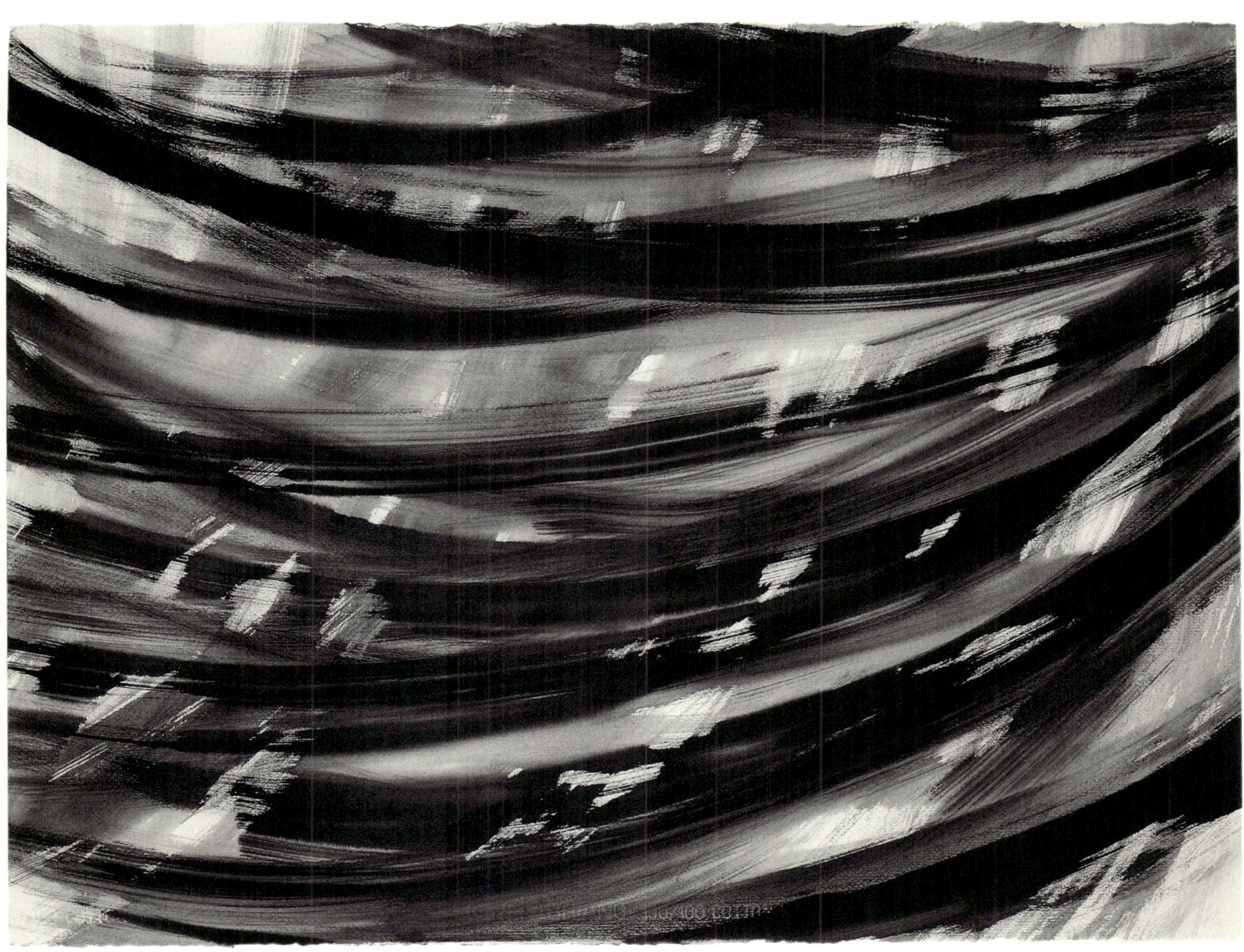

PLATE IV

Untitled 11, 2001

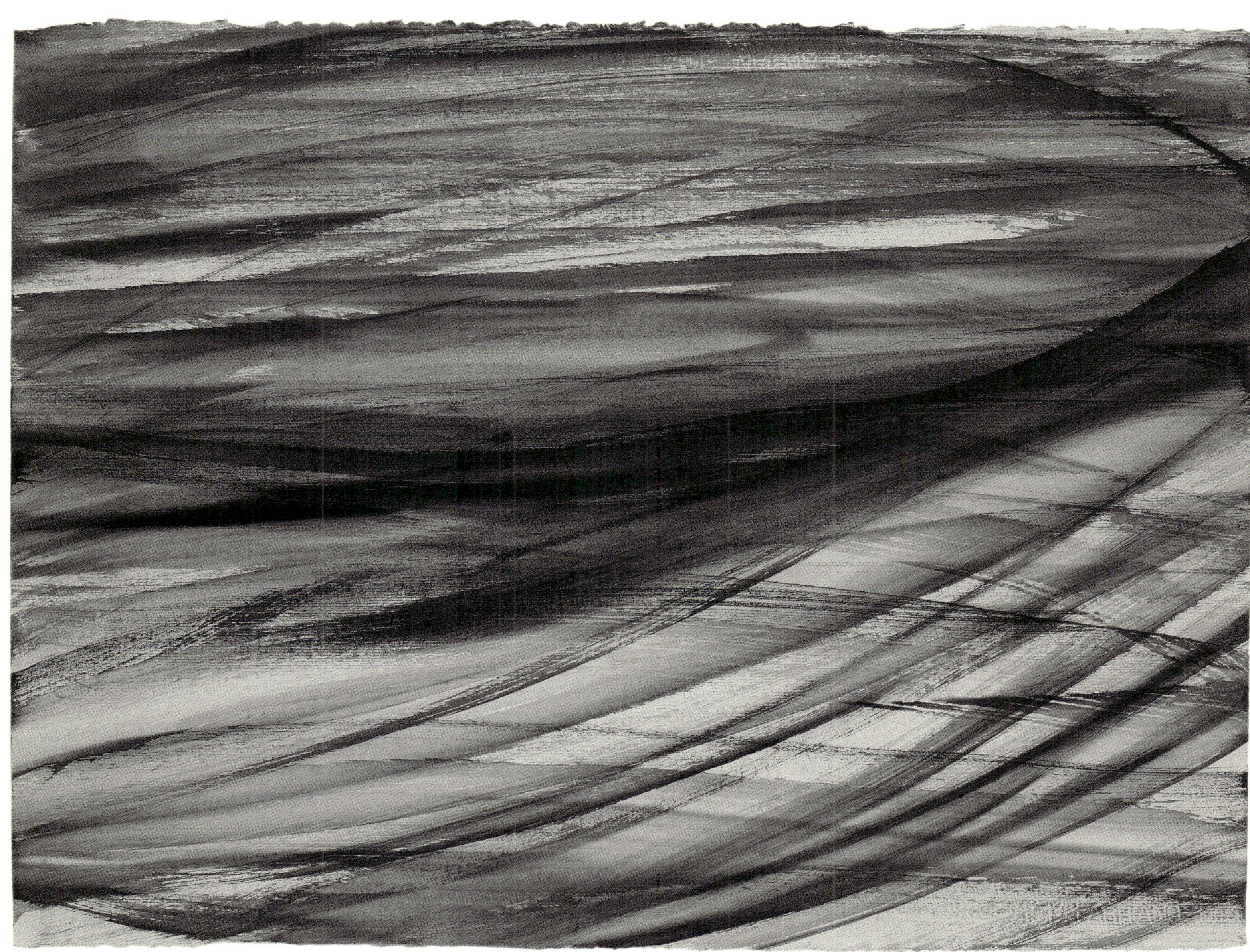

PLATE V

Untitled 8, 2001

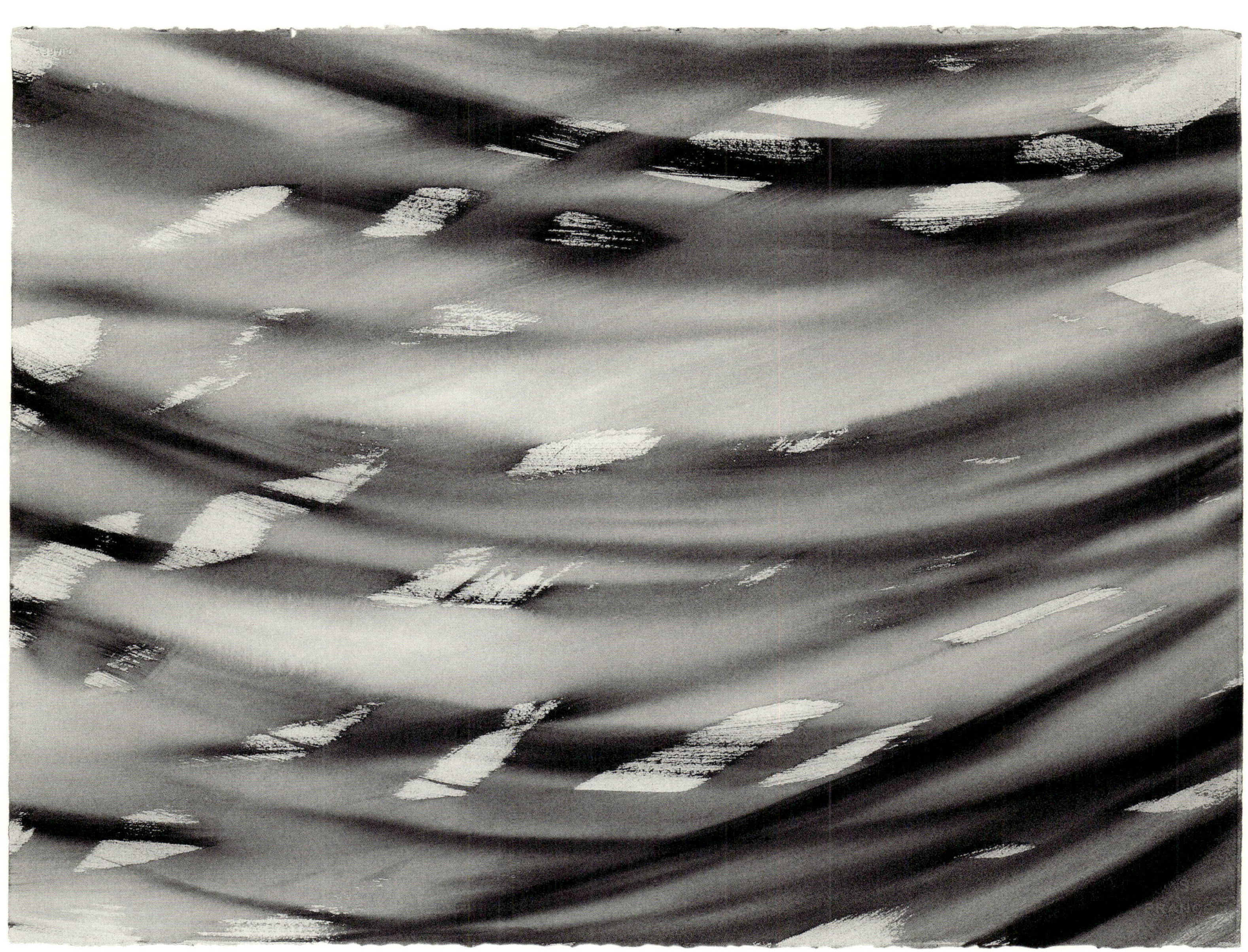

PLATE VI

Untitled 12, 2000–2001

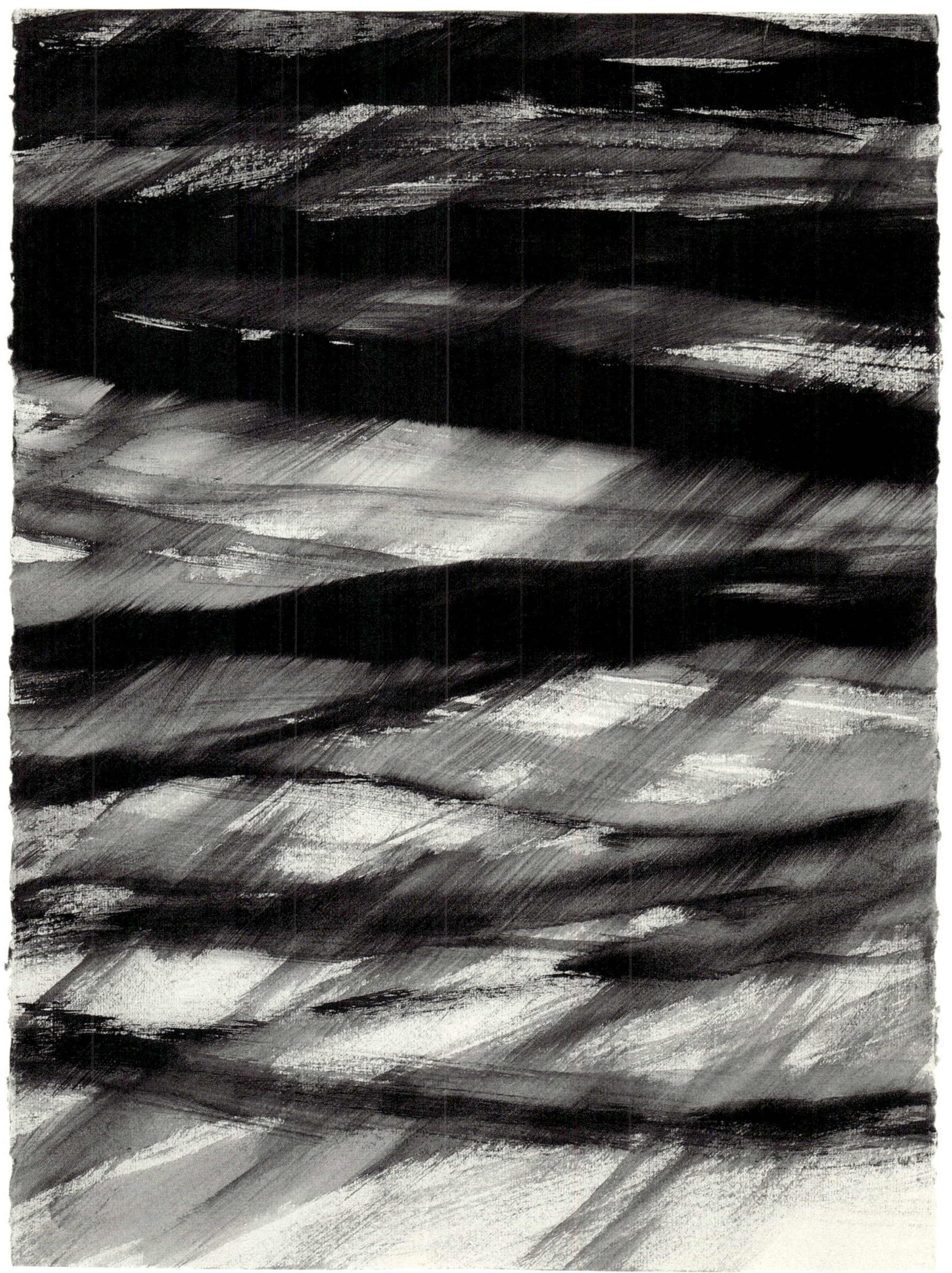

PLATE VII

Untitled 9, 2001

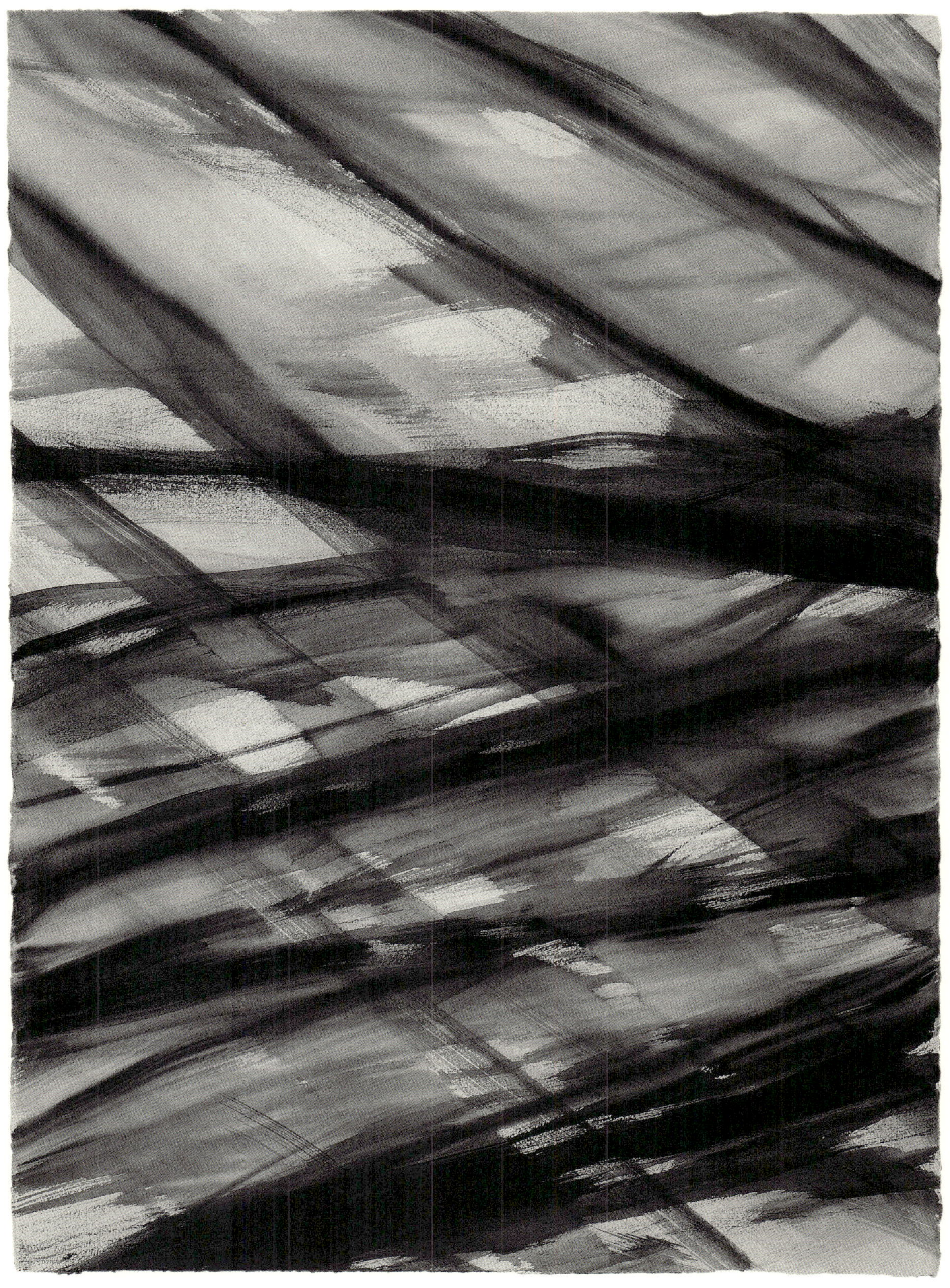

PLATE VIII

Untitled 14, 2000–2001

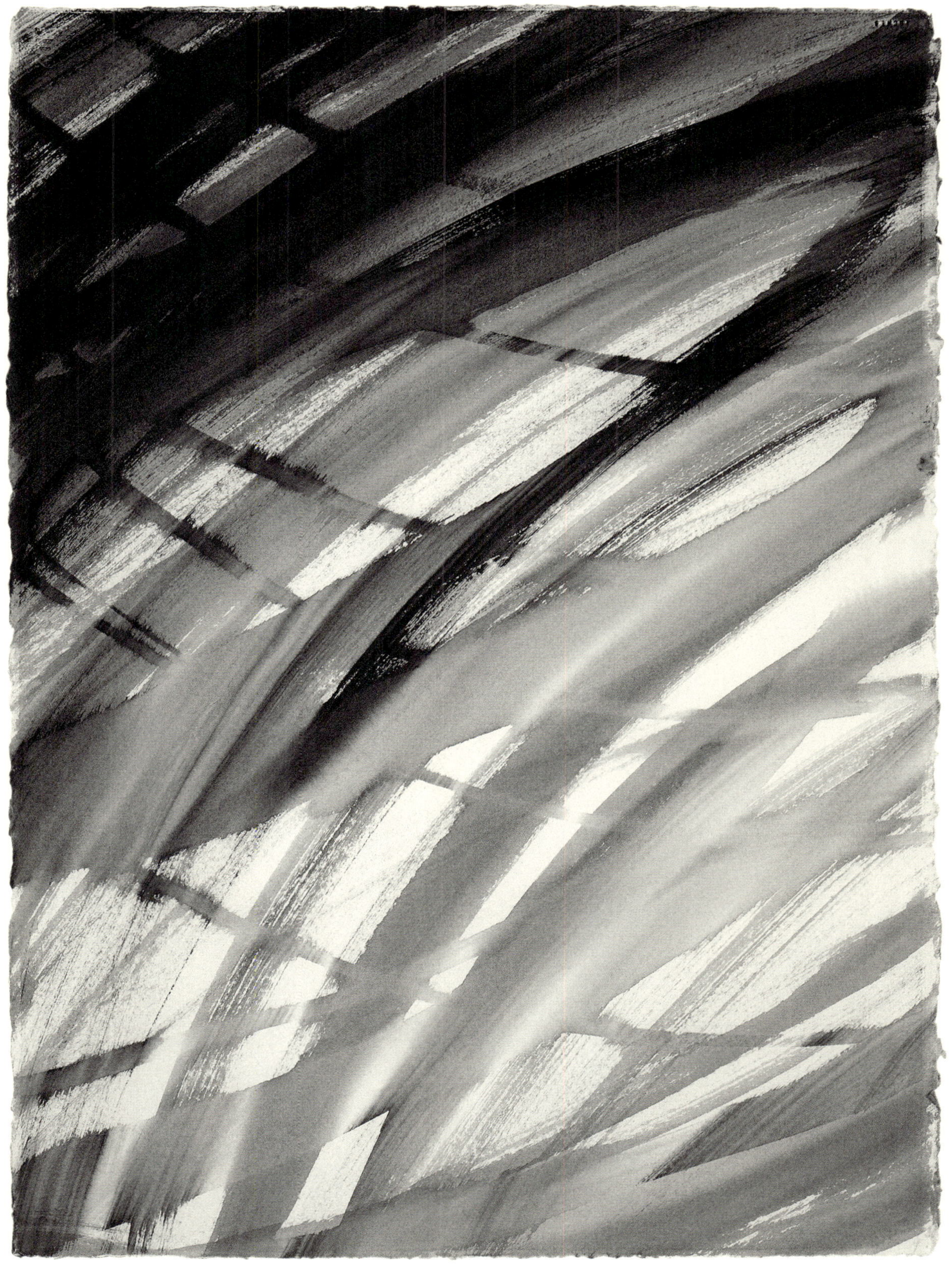

PLATE IX

Untitled 10, 2000–2001

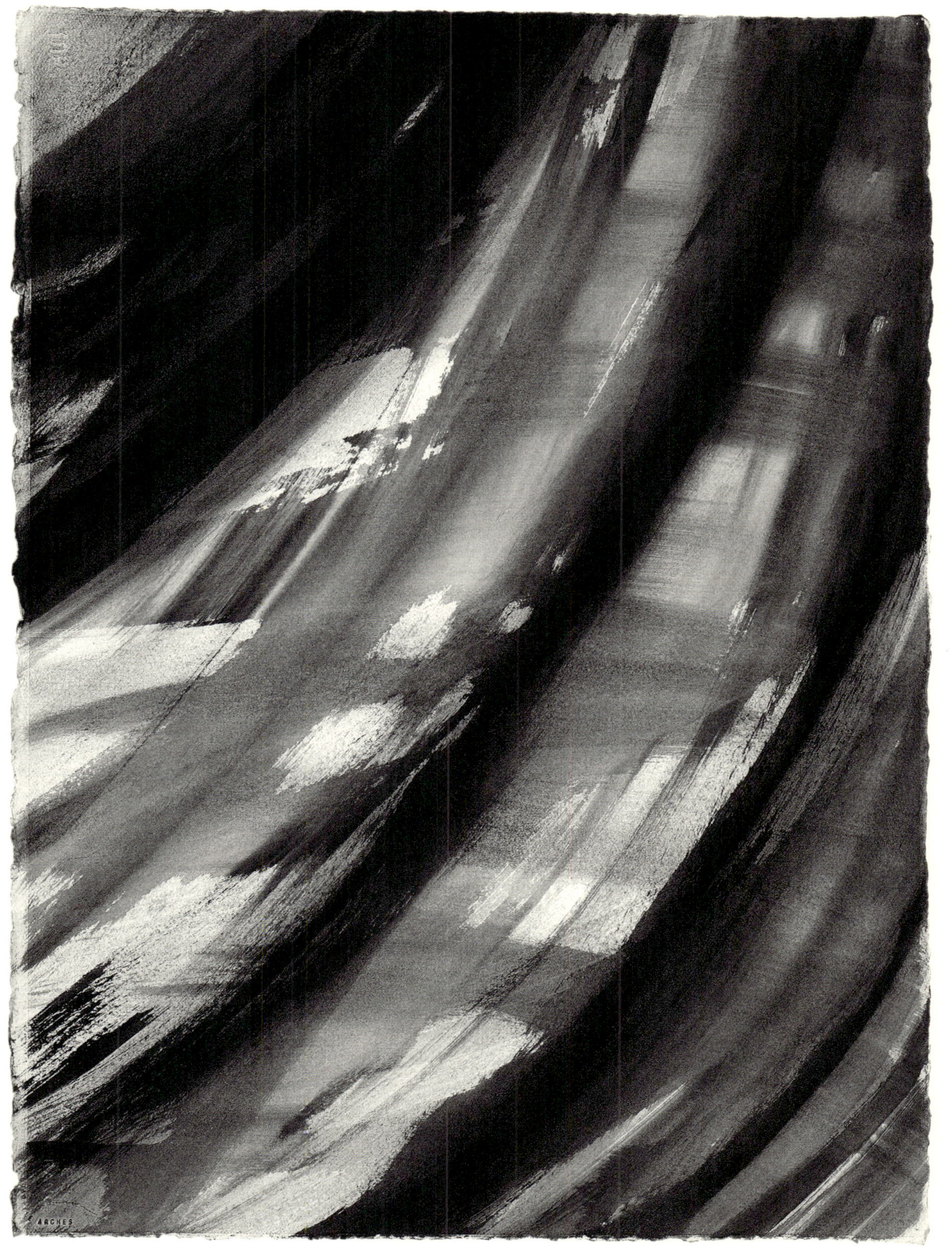

PLATE X

Untitled 6, 2000–2001

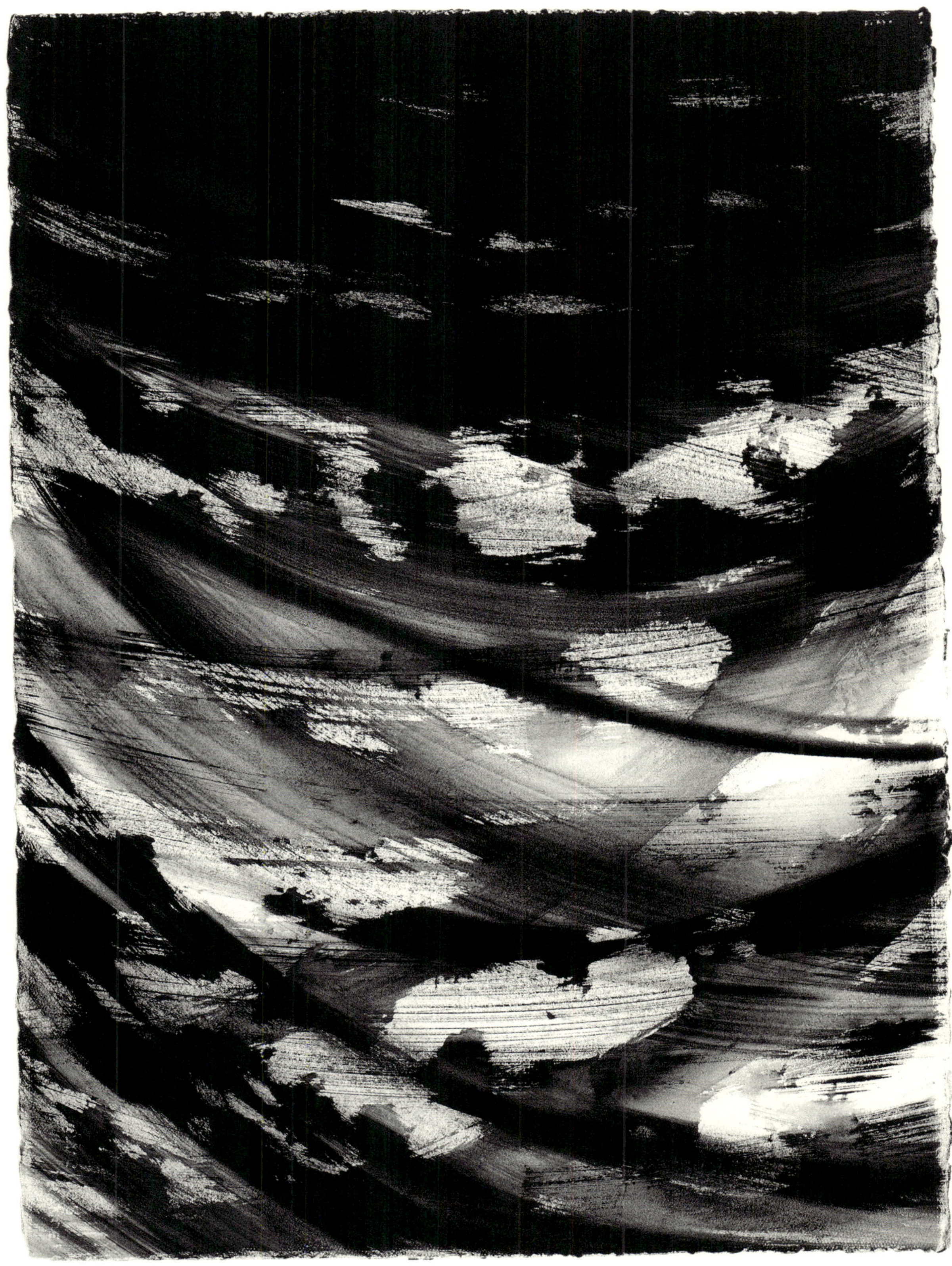

PLATE XI

Untitled 4, 2001

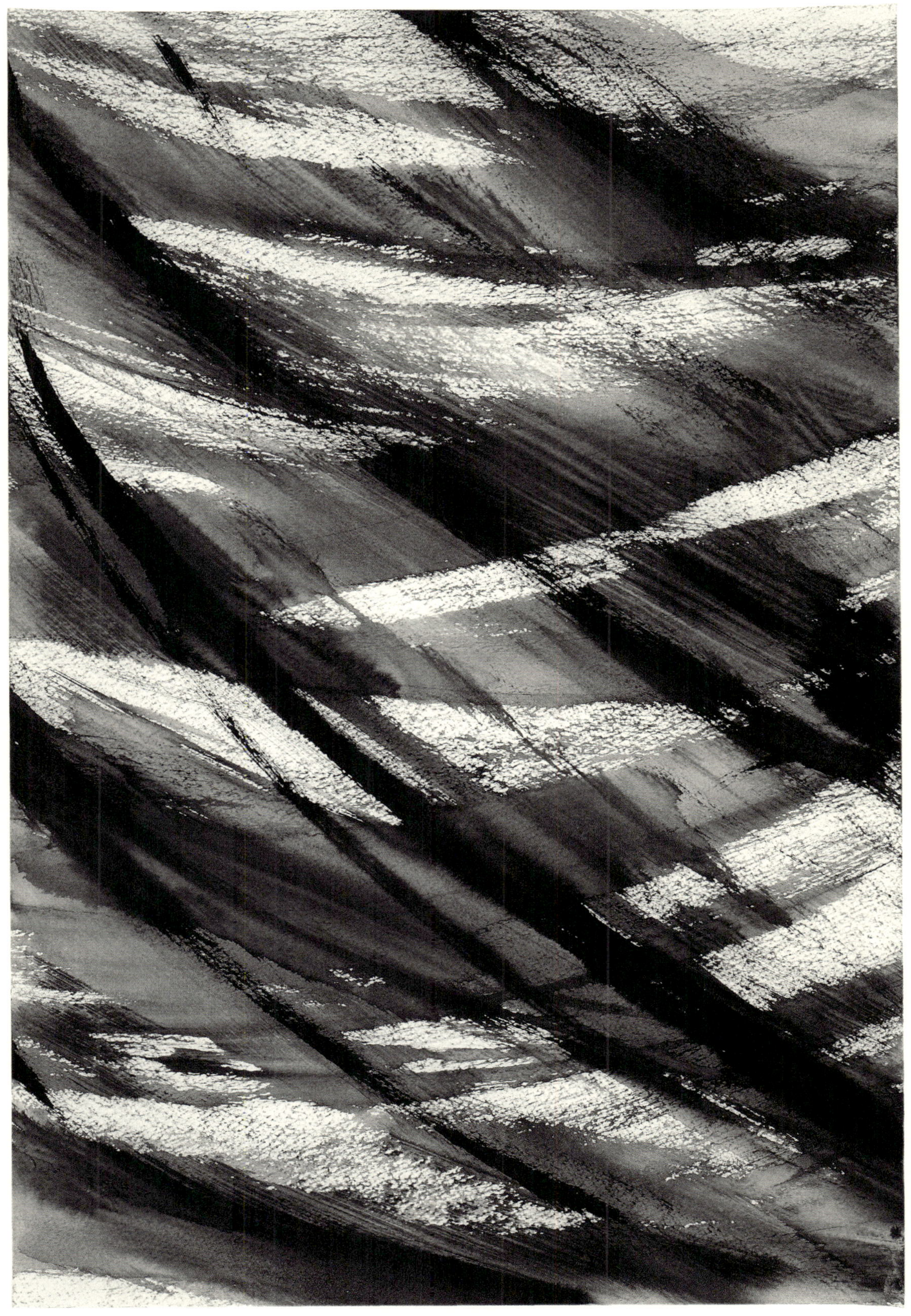

PLATE XII

Untitled 3, 2001

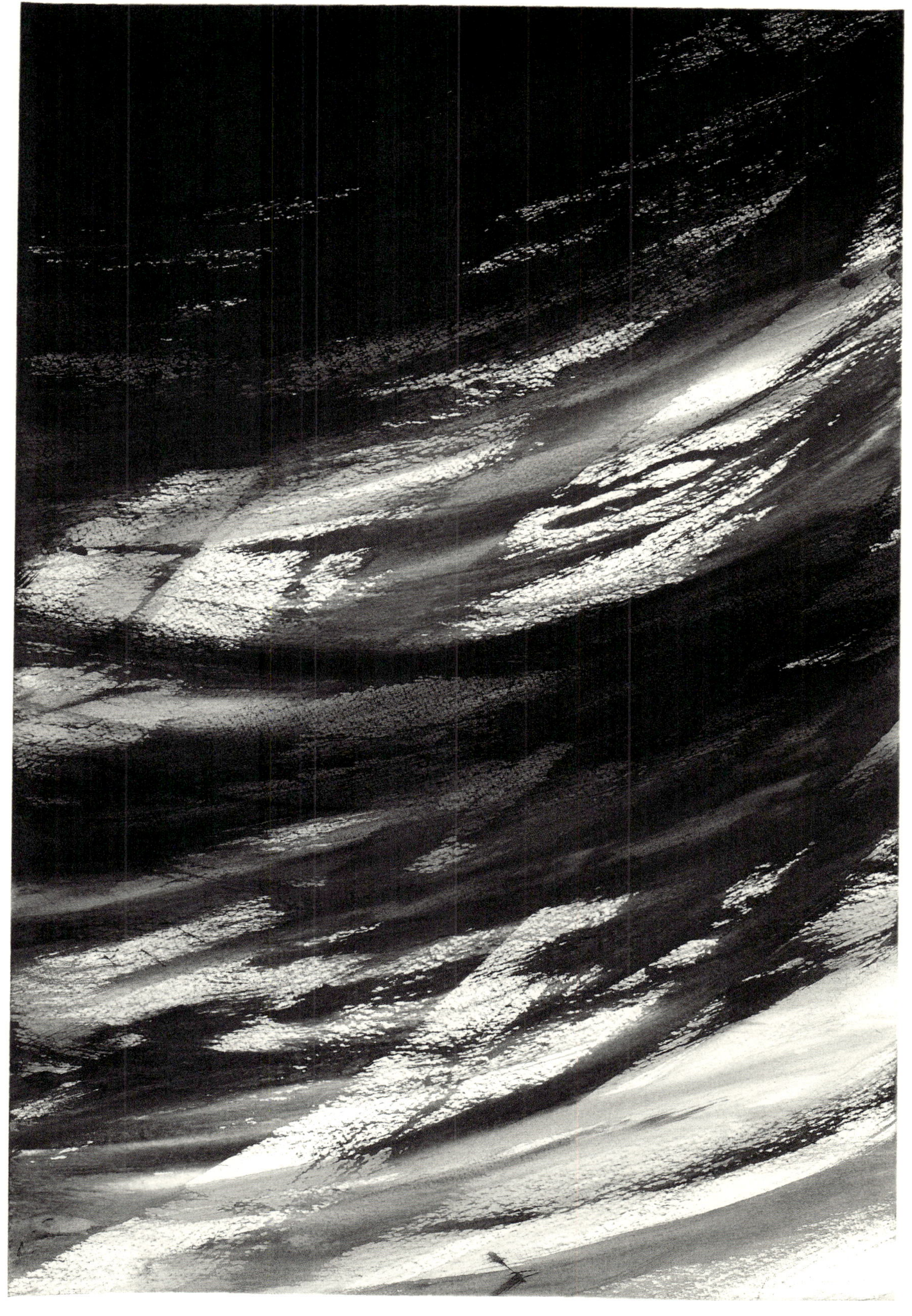

PLATE XIII

Riverrun, 2001

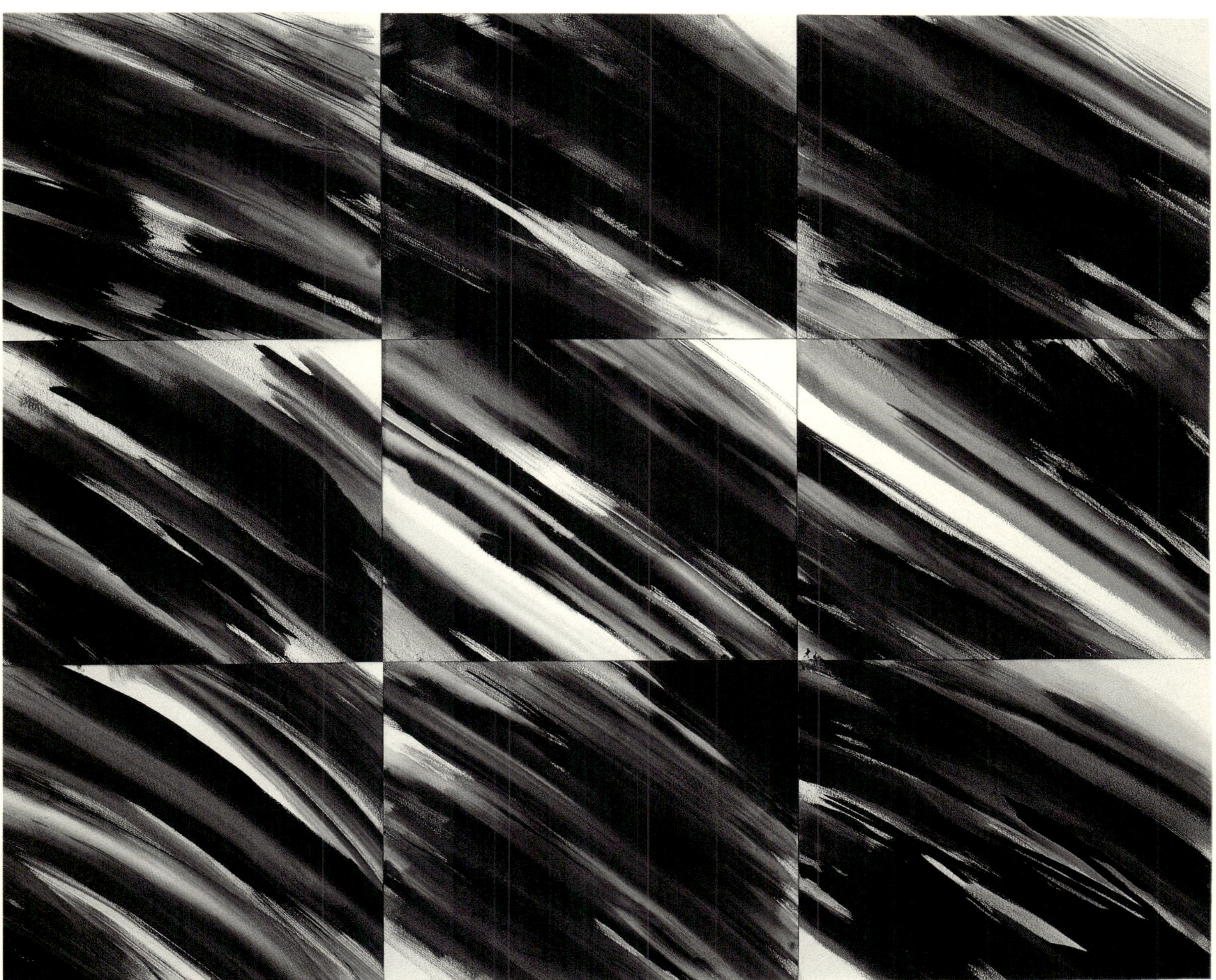

NEW DRAWINGS BY ELYN ZIMMERMAN

by Pepe Karmel

For anyone familiar with her earlier work, Elyn Zimmerman's new drawings will come as something of a shock. As much as her work has evolved over the last quarter-century, it has always been marked by an instantly recognizable combination of power, elegance, and serenity — qualities equally evident in her massive stone installations and her deceptively simple drawings and photographs. Now, suddenly, in these drawings done between fall 2000 and summer 2001, she has burst into a new realm of expression. Serenity has given way to emotion; controlled design has been replaced by what seems like spontaneous gesture. The drawings appear, at first glance, almost the work of a different artist. On closer study, however, they reveal many of the same concerns that have shaped Zimmerman's art throughout its trajectory.

* * *

Speaking broadly, Zimmerman's subject has always been the relationship between art and nature. Her earliest installations explored the use of artificial materials to reproduce seemingly "natural" phenomena of refraction and reflection. Her later installations have reversed this process, using natural materials to produce the heightened awareness of light, texture, and mass that we usually associate with painting and sculpture. Interrogating the difference between artificial and natural signs, her drawings and photographs have addressed the same concerns *within* the realm of representation.

Detail from *Untitled 8*, 2001

Born in Philadelphia in 1945, Zimmerman studied art and perceptual psychology at UCLA, where she became part of the circle of "Light and Space" artists including James Turrell, Robert Irwin, and Maria Nordman. Her first one-person exhibition, in 1974, included a sculpture made from eight rectangular strips of glass leaning in a row against a wall, illuminated by quartz lights positioned at right and left (opposite). Seen head on, the glass strips were transparent, but the light angling through them was refracted so they cast a fan-shaped array of shadows on the wall. The glass was solid and the shadows were not, but, visually, the shadows carried more weight.

Another 1974 work, *Equivalent Abstractions* (pages 8-9), also probed the trustworthiness of visual experience. A series of photographs traced the progress of a beam of light, falling from a clerestory window and moving across an empty studio space (page 10). These photographs were then reproduced in a series of meticulously shaded graphite drawings (page 11). Hung one above the other, the two series challenged the viewer to distinguish between the supposedly "objective" medium of photography and the supposedly "subjective" medium of drawing. In *Equivalent Abstraction: Roma Window* (pages 46-47), an even more dramatic pairing of photographs and drawings, the camera-eye seemed to stare with unblinking intensity at the position of the setting sun; instead of the sun descending toward the horizon, it was the high mullioned window that moved up and out of the picture frame.

Untitled, 1974
Eight glass panels, two quartz lights, each panel measures 8′ x 1′ x ¼″
Elyn Zimmerman,
May 15 – June 23, 1974
University of California,
Berkeley Art Museum

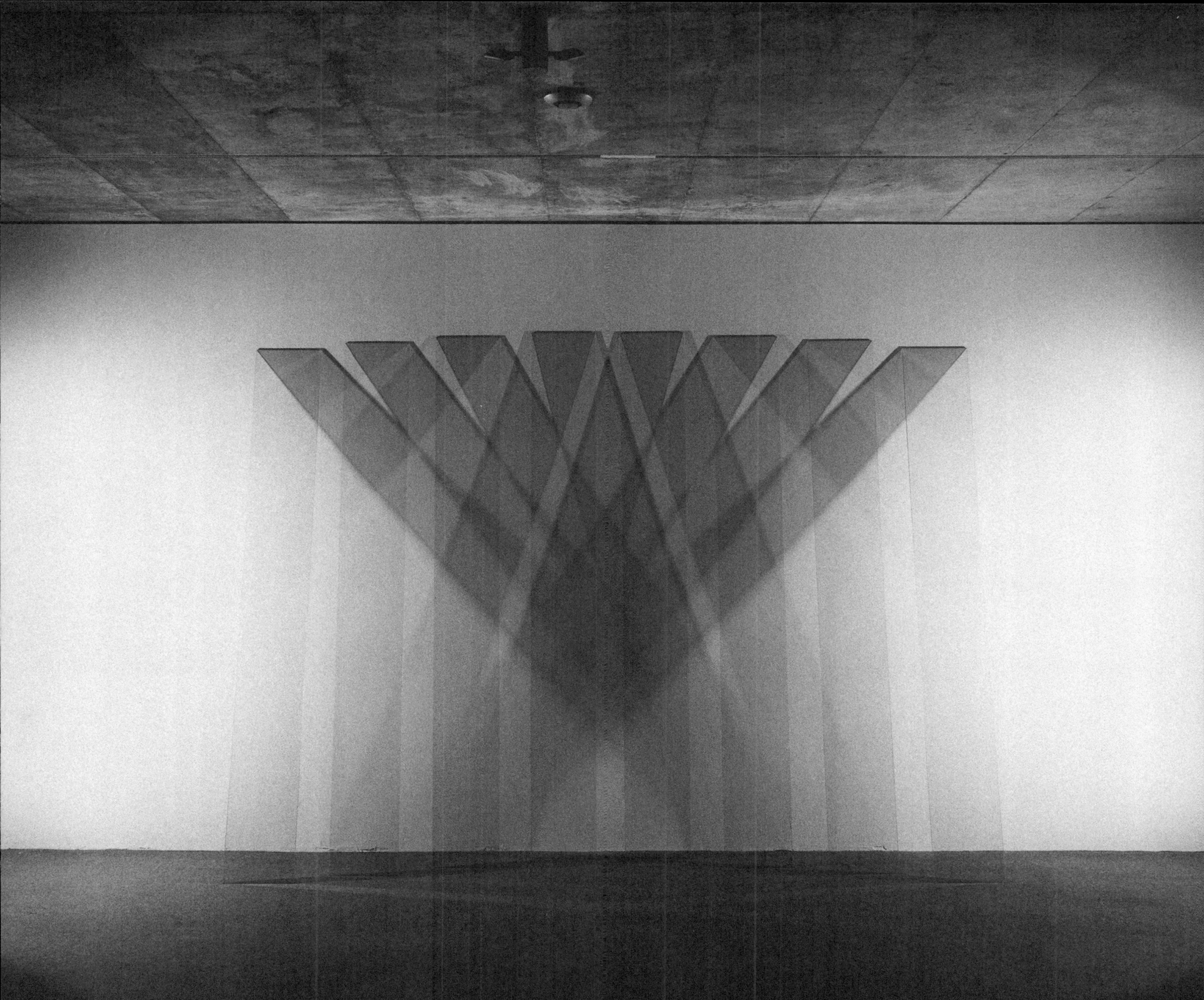

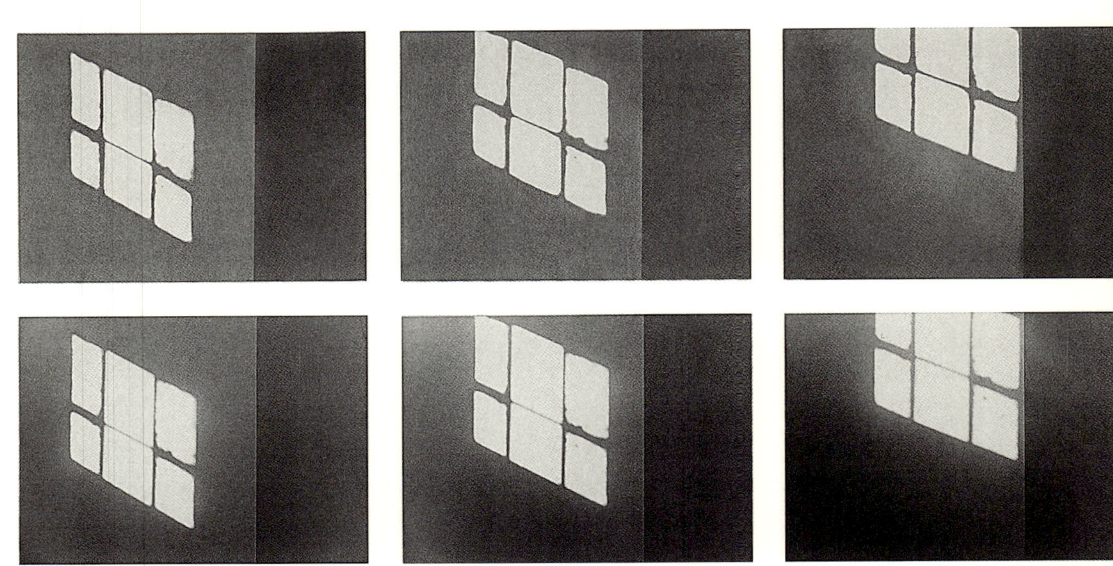

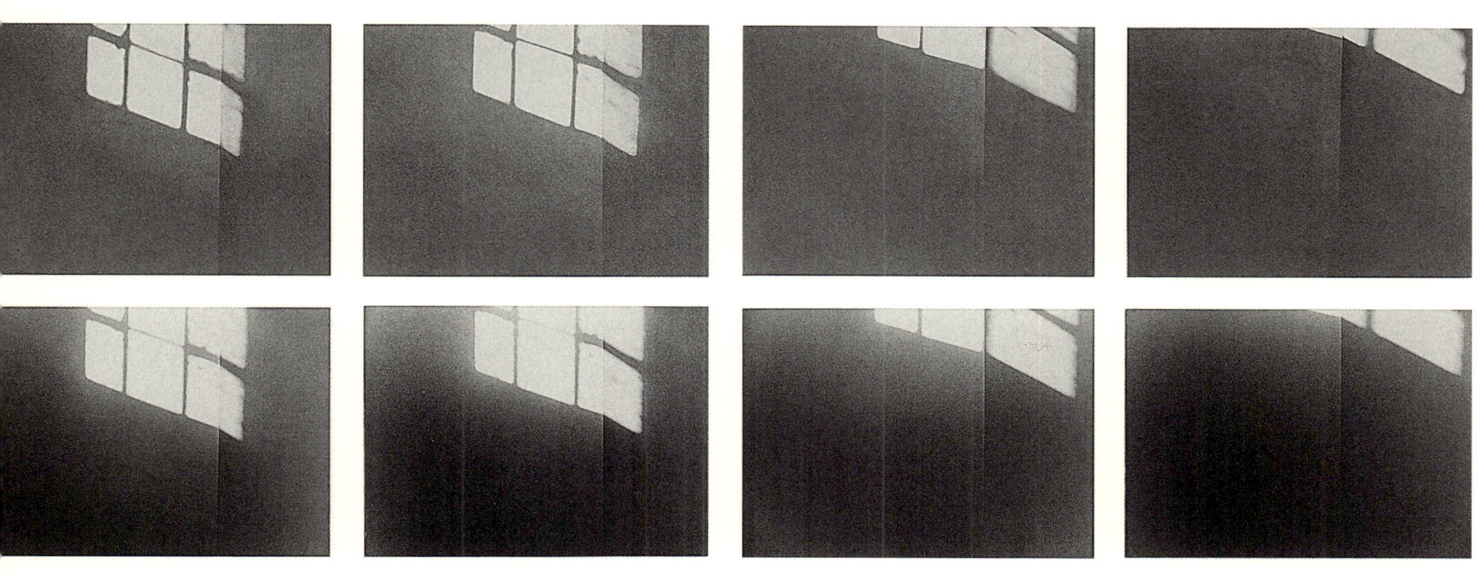

Equivalent Abstraction: Roma Window, 1975
7 gelatin silver prints each 14½″ x 19½″ and 7 graphite drawings each 14½″ x 19½″
Private Collection

Five years later, at the Museum of Contemporary Art, in Chicago, Zimmerman constructed a *Black Pool* within a darkened room; a column, brilliantly illuminated, rose from the center of the shallow pool, merging with its reflection in the dark water (opposite). Already-existing architectural features (the column, track lights) combined with an element borrowed from nature (water) to produce an experience of almost spiritual intensity, recalling the sacred enclosures of Indian temples.

Black Pool II, 1979
Pool 60′ l x 6′ w x 6″ d and
2 focussing spotlights
Museum of Contemporary Art,
Chicago, Illinois

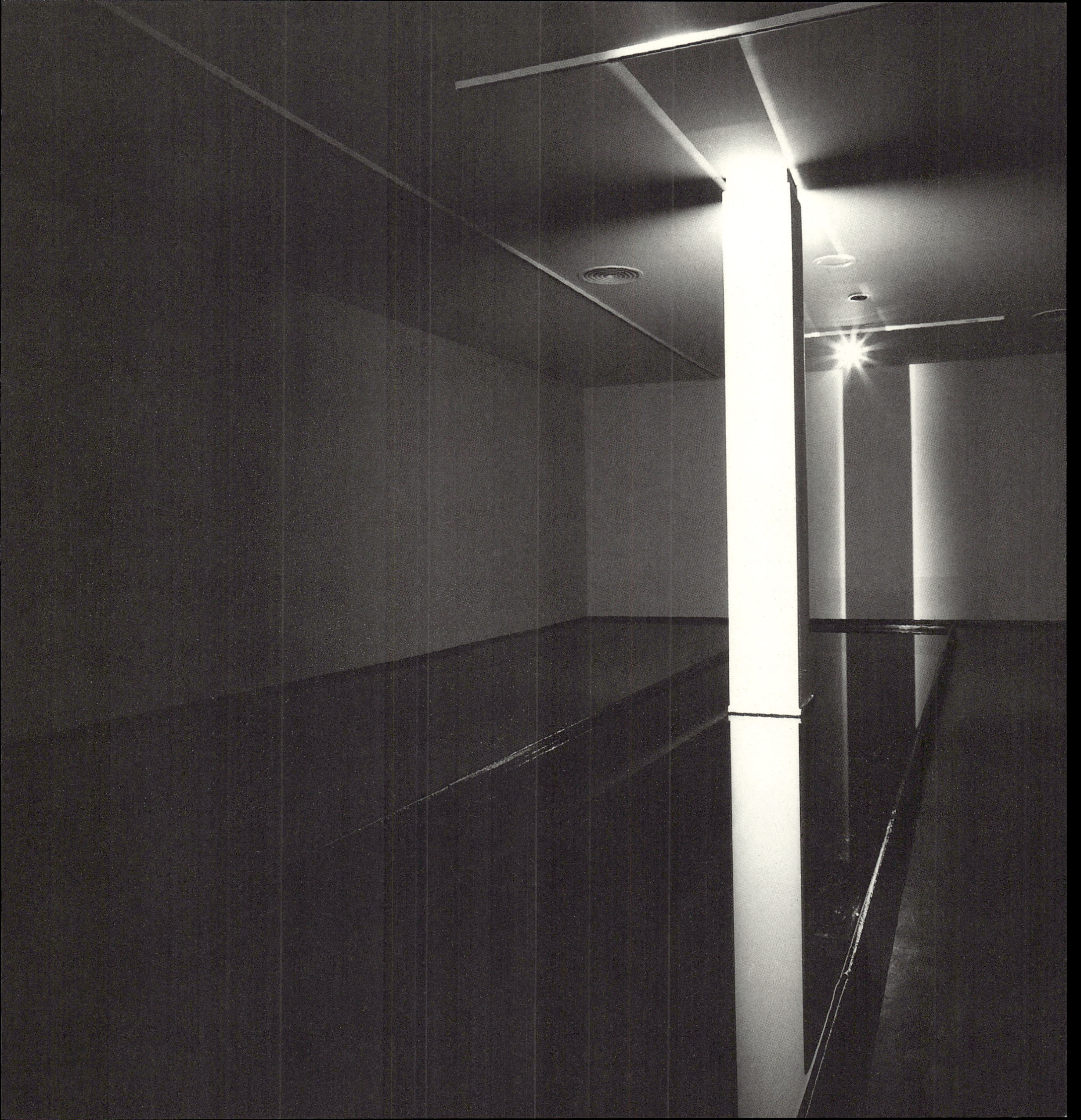

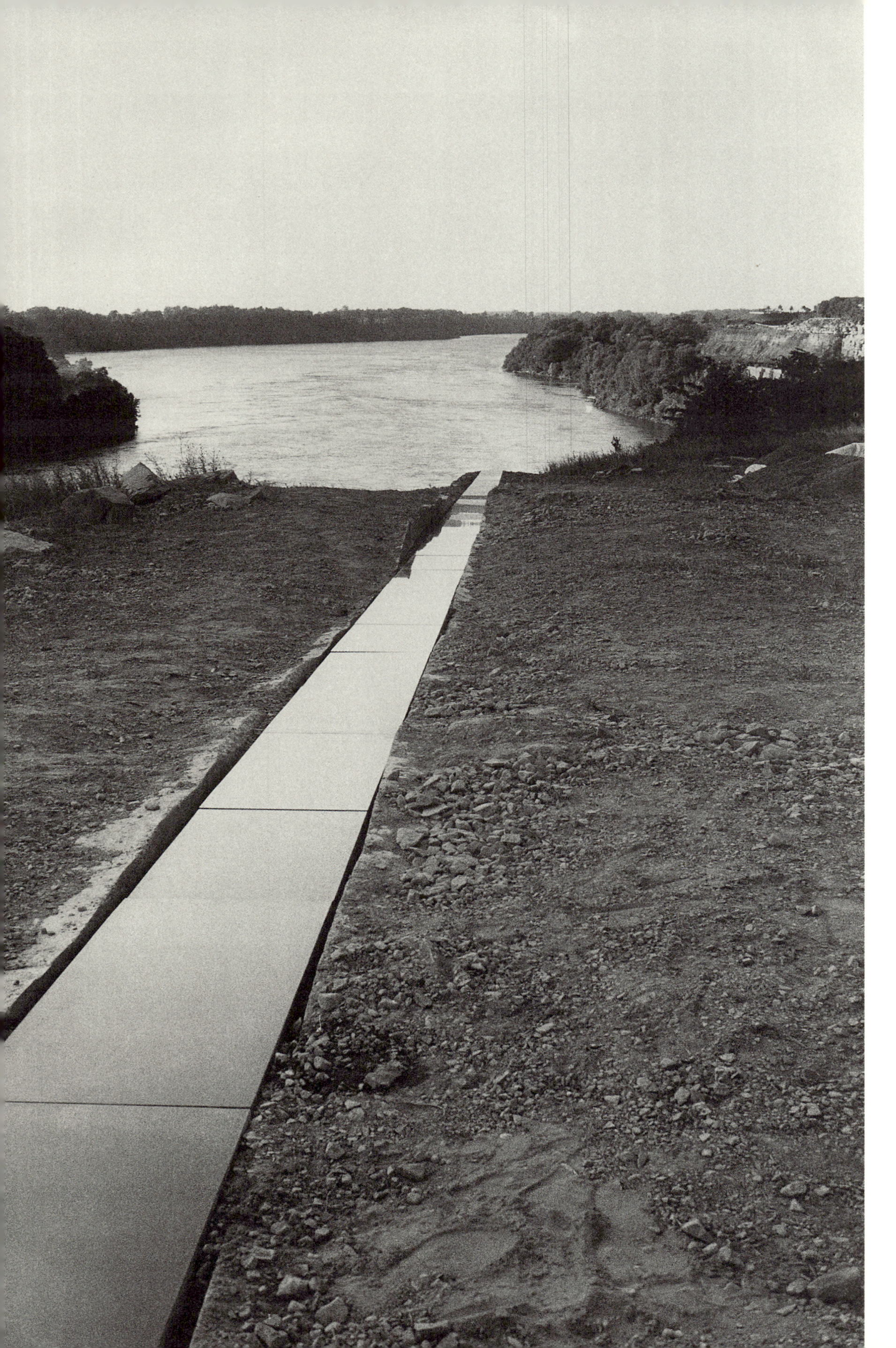

Indeed, Zimmerman had visited India in 1977, where her career received a decisive impetus from the temples at Ellora and Ajanta, carved into the living rock of cliff sides. Here, the raw material of the unfinished stone remained visible, side-by-side with the sculpture and "masonry" carved from it. One year later, Zimmerman constructed *Monarch's Trough*: a strip of polished granite, two feet wide and one hundred fifty feet long, sunk into the top of a cliff overlooking the turbulent waters of the Niagara Gorge (opposite). Reflecting the sky and clouds passing overhead, the polished stone seemed more like water, running through a trough towards cliff's edge and spilling over into the river below.

Monarch's Trough, 1978
Polished granite 2′ w x 150′ l x 2″ d
Artpark, Niagara Gorge, Lewiston, New York

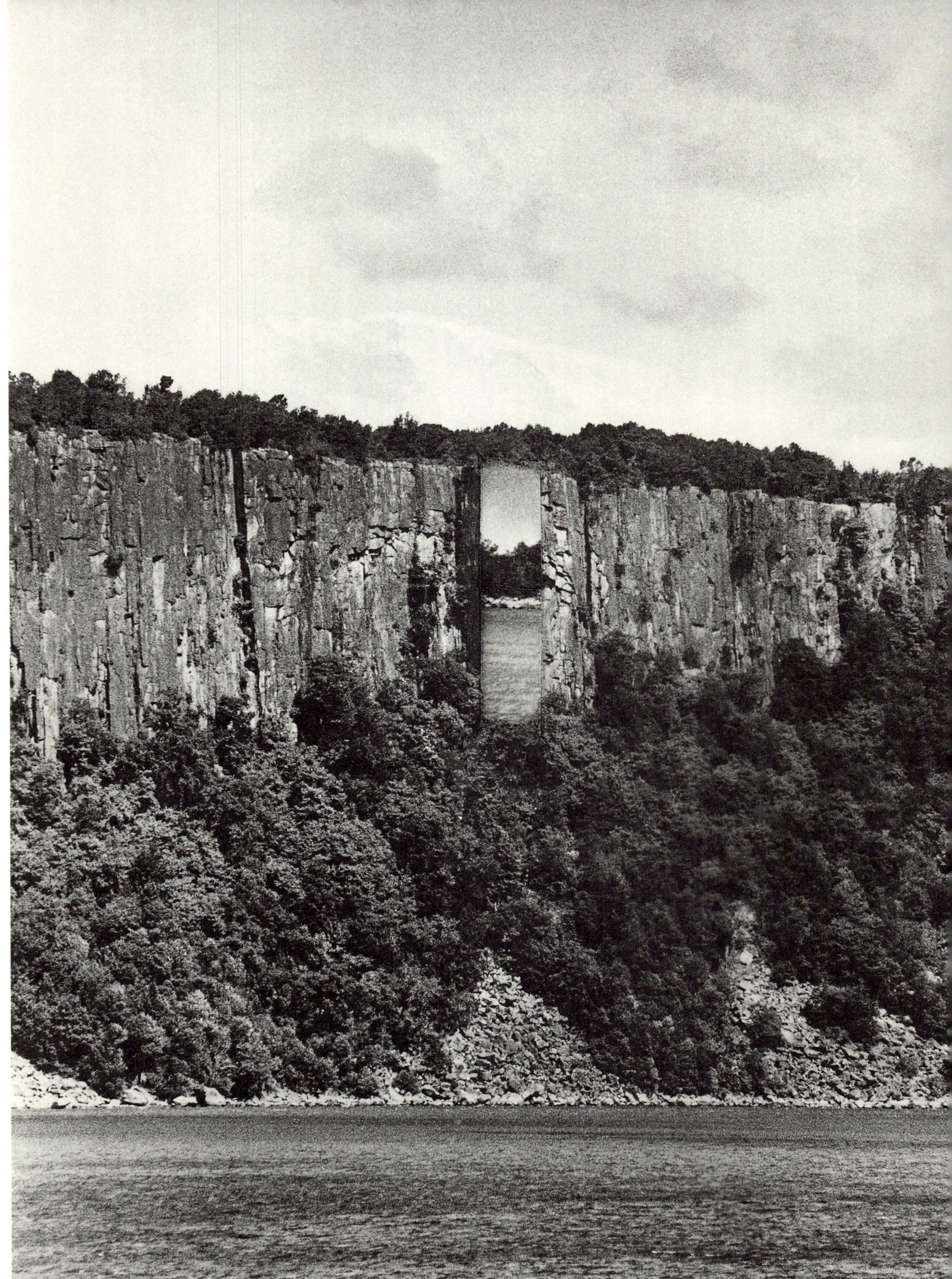

In her *Palisades Project* of 1981 (opposite), Zimmerman proposed erecting an even larger strip of polished granite on the west bank of the Hudson River, dividing the uneven cliff-faces of the Palisades and forming a visual liaison between the river below and the sky above. The *Equivalent Abstractions* had juxtaposed two man-made media; the *Palisades Project* proposed a far grander confrontation between natural elements: rock, water, and air. In its natural form, the rock of the cliff face echoed the undulations of the water below, but not its mobility or reflectiveness. In its polished form, the rock became a reflecting surface, borrowing the luminosity of the sky and the mobility of the clouds, but at the cost of giving up its original, uneven contours. By a (conceptually) simple intervention, Zimmerman subverted the perceptual categories dividing stone from water, water from air, the natural from the unnatural.

Palisades Project, 1981
Photomontage proposal

Monarch's Trough also provided the jumping-off point for the remarkable series of sculptures and installations that Zimmerman has executed over the last twenty years. Perhaps the best-known of these is *Marabar*, created in 1984 for the plaza in front of the National Geographic Society in Washington, D.C. (opposite). Here, a long reflecting pool is ringed by massive boulders, some encroaching on the pool, some retreating from it, and others stopping short at its edge. If the proportions of the pool recall the artificial *Black Pool* of 1979, its wind-ruffled surface evokes the flowing waters of the Hudson. While the overall contours of the boulders appear natural, three of them have had faces sheared away and polished to mirror smoothness. Having created her own natural environment, Zimmerman can subvert it without guilt, creating an endless play of mirrors—between the boulders that face each other across the pool, and between the categories we impose on the world around us.

Marabar, 1984
Plaza design National Geographic Society Headquarters, Washington, D.C.
Natural cleft and polished granite blocks, varying sizes
Pool 60′ l x 6′ w x 16″ d and adjacent landscape

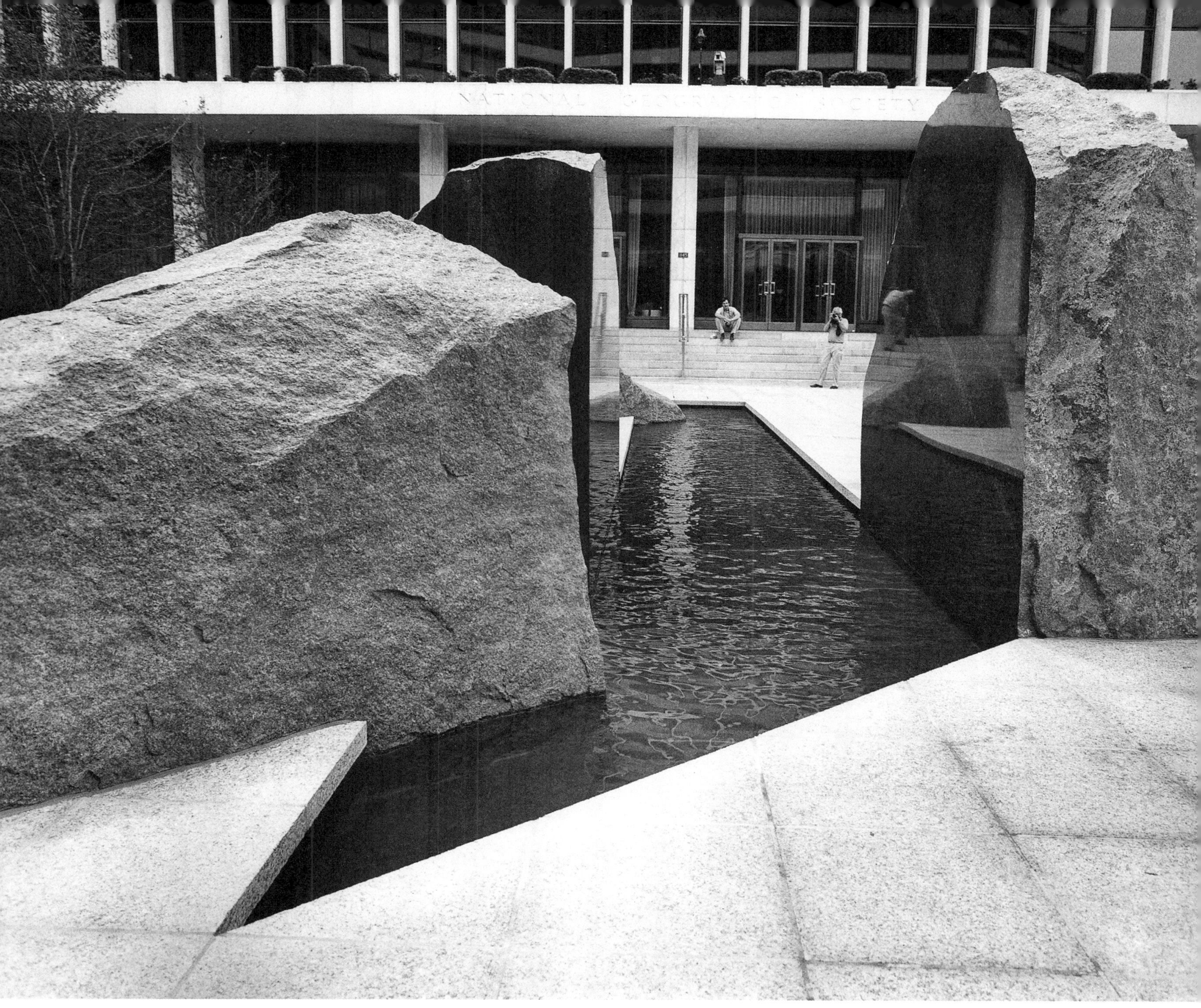
NATIONAL

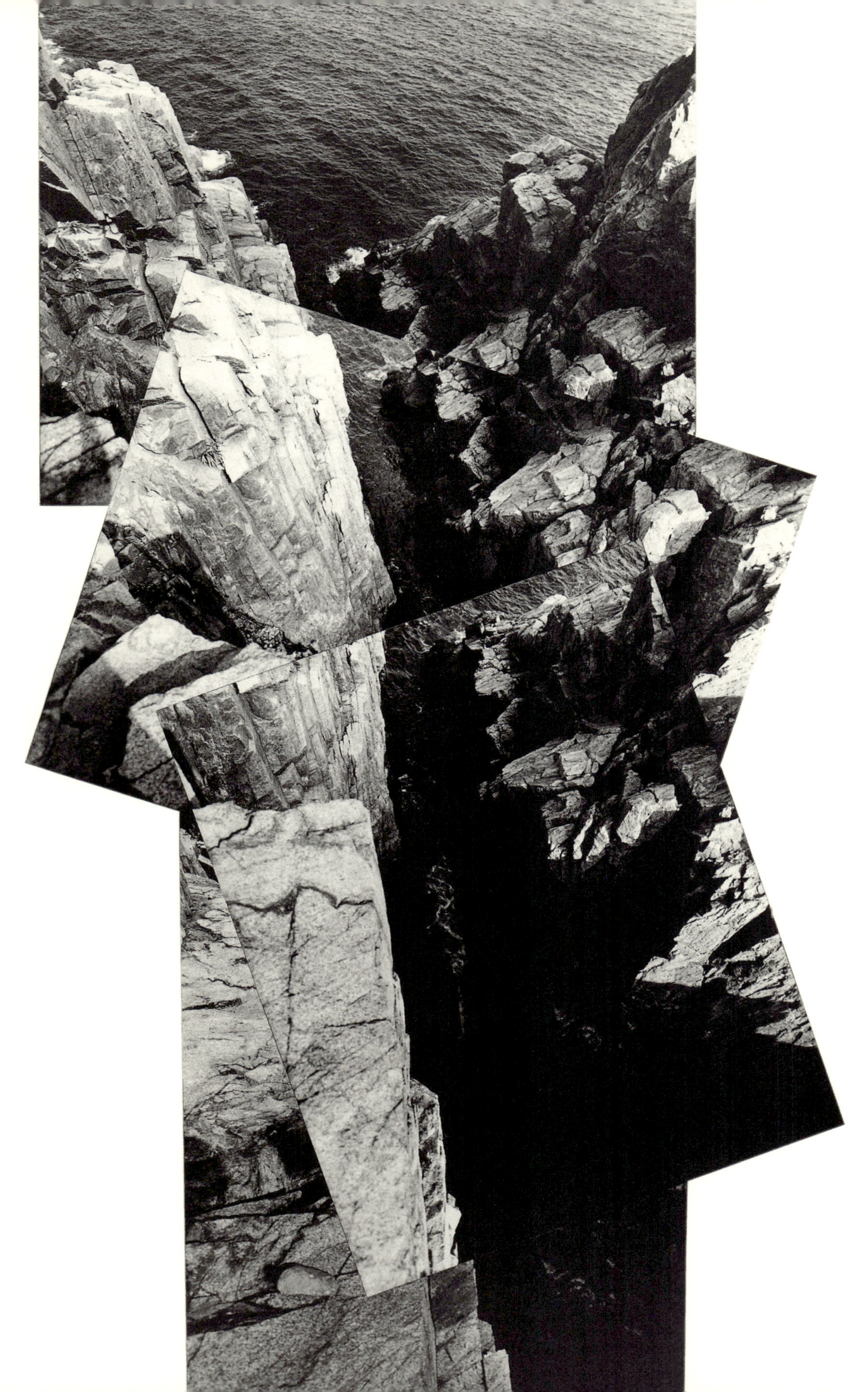

Zimmerman's numerous sculptural projects have not kept her from creating remarkable works in other media. Some of these, like the photographic portrait of an inlet in *Mount Desert, Maine* (opposite), address the same elements—rock, water, and light—found in her sculpture. Here, a series of detailed, overlapping prints allows Zimmerman to describe the natural terrain with tenacious specificity, while extending the breadth (or, more precisely, height) of the view beyond the borders of a conventional photograph. Rotating from vertical to horizontal, the prints force the viewer's eye to remain in motion, while their overlapping edges echo the fracture lines of the rocks they depict.

Other pictures explore the artificial gorges of the city (pages 58-59). Zimmerman's *Cityscapes* take their place in a tradition reaching back to Alfred Stieglitz's photographs of New York skyscrapers, taken in the early 1930s. But where Stieglitz's skyscrapers rise like fantastical temples, with every cornice, molding, or girder crisply outlined by sunlight and shadow, Zimmerman moves her camera to create a sense of architecture in motion. The sunlit peaks of office towers detach themselves and float away into the sky, while the cornices of older buildings shoot sideways, leaving dark trails behind them. In Zimmerman's hands, photography ceases to be a sober means of documentation, and becomes instead a keyboard for composing tone-poems about the city.

Landscape Study: Mt. Desert, Maine, 1986
Gelatin silver print montage, 54″ x 29″

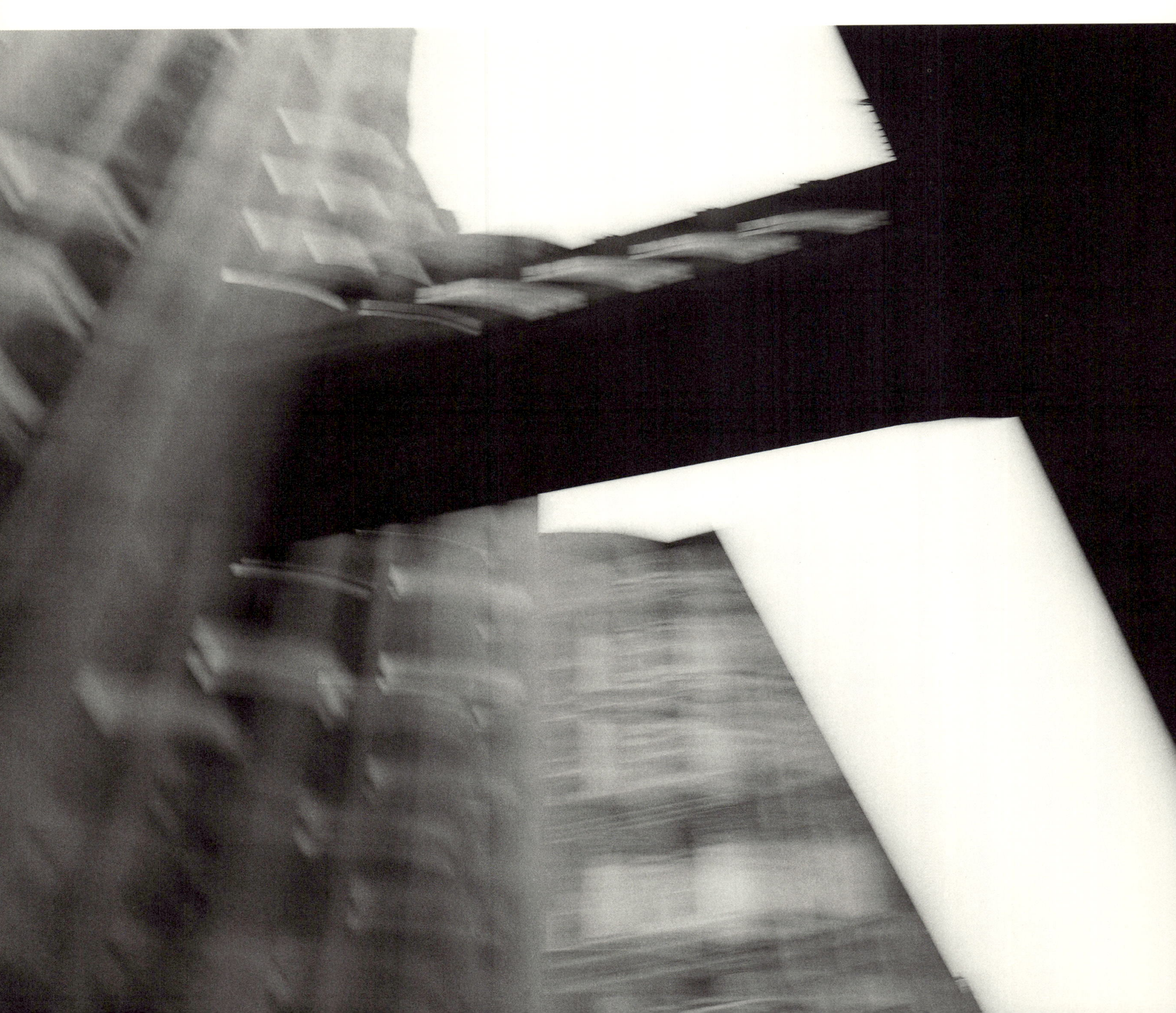

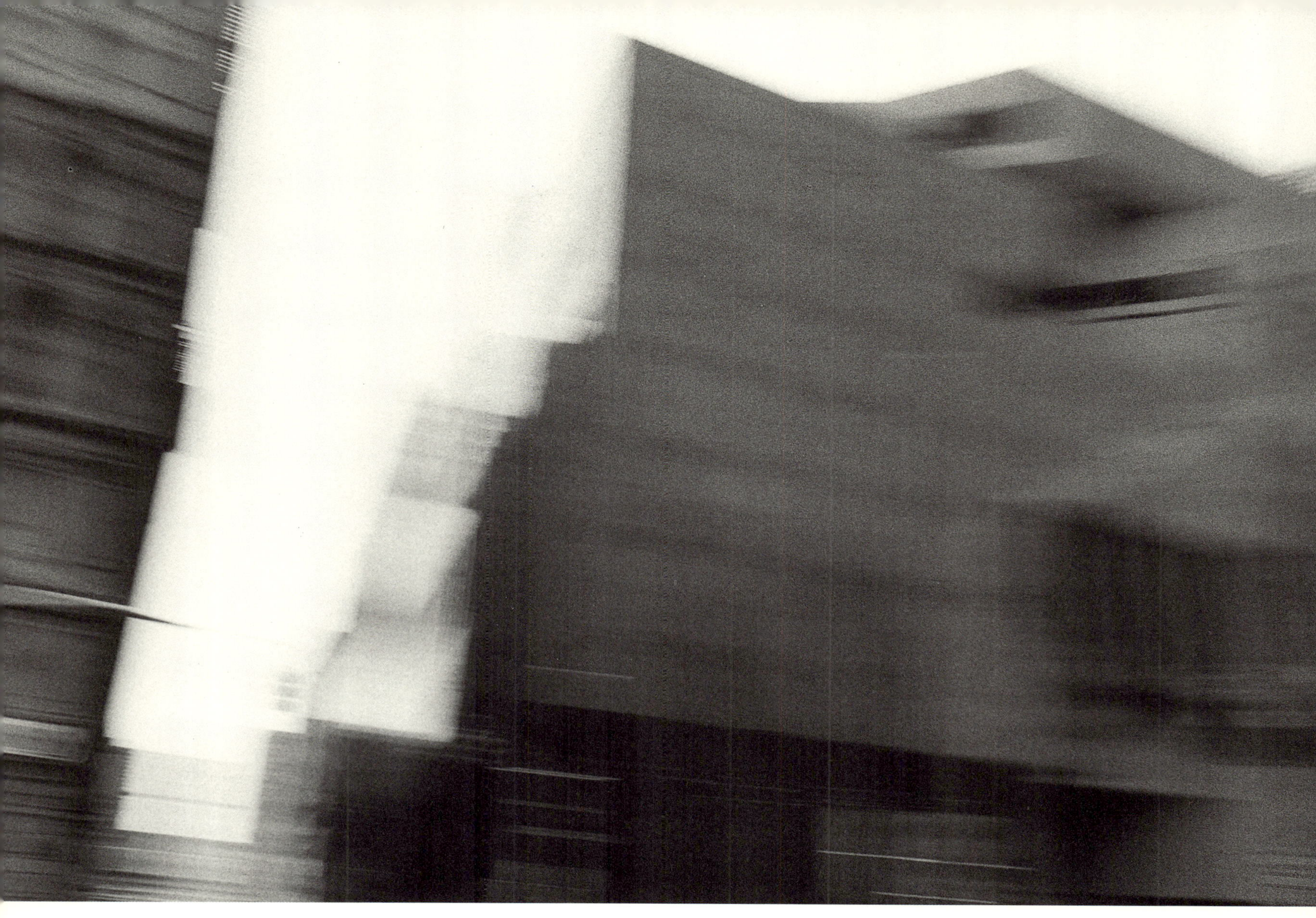

Both pages:
Untitled Cityscape, 1980
Gelatin silver print, 36" x 42"
Private Collection

The point of departure for Zimmerman's most recent work is a sculpture, *Tetra*, that she designed in 1999-2000 for the garden of a private collector (opposite). Here, four rough-cut pylons rise within a circular pool, surrounding a polished granite drum supported by four smooth-faced cubes. Water emerges from the flat top of the drum, descends its sides in a continuous sheet, and then goes into free fall, raising small whitecaps where it encounters the surface of the pool below. The force of the impact creates a series of ripples that spread outward through the apertures between the cubes and the pylons. As they approach the circumference of the pool, the spreading ripples from each pair of apertures meet and form a series of overlapping waves (page 63) — the kind of "interference pattern" that high-school students learn about in physics class. Zimmerman had not foreseen this effect, but as she oversaw the completion of the actual sculpture, it began irresistibly to attract her attention.

That fall, when she went to Vermont for a residency at an artists' colony, she found herself impelled to respond in a different medium to the experience of the sculpture. She began by making a group of photographs recording the passage of water through the shallow bed of a nearby stream (page 68). In certain of these, intersecting ripples formed an "interference pattern" similar to the patterns she had discovered in *Tetra*; but the play of light and shade overhead disguised this regular pattern, breaking some of the surface into interlocking patches of black and white, and merging the rest into a continuous expanse of shimmering silver (page 4). In other photographs, rocks and pebbles below the surface interrupted the regular patterns of the ripples, creating jostling areas of turbulence, frozen into narrow veins of light and dark (page 13).

Tetra, 1999–2000
Natural cleft and polished granite, water
9′ h x 18′ diameter
Marie-Josée and Henry Kravis Collection

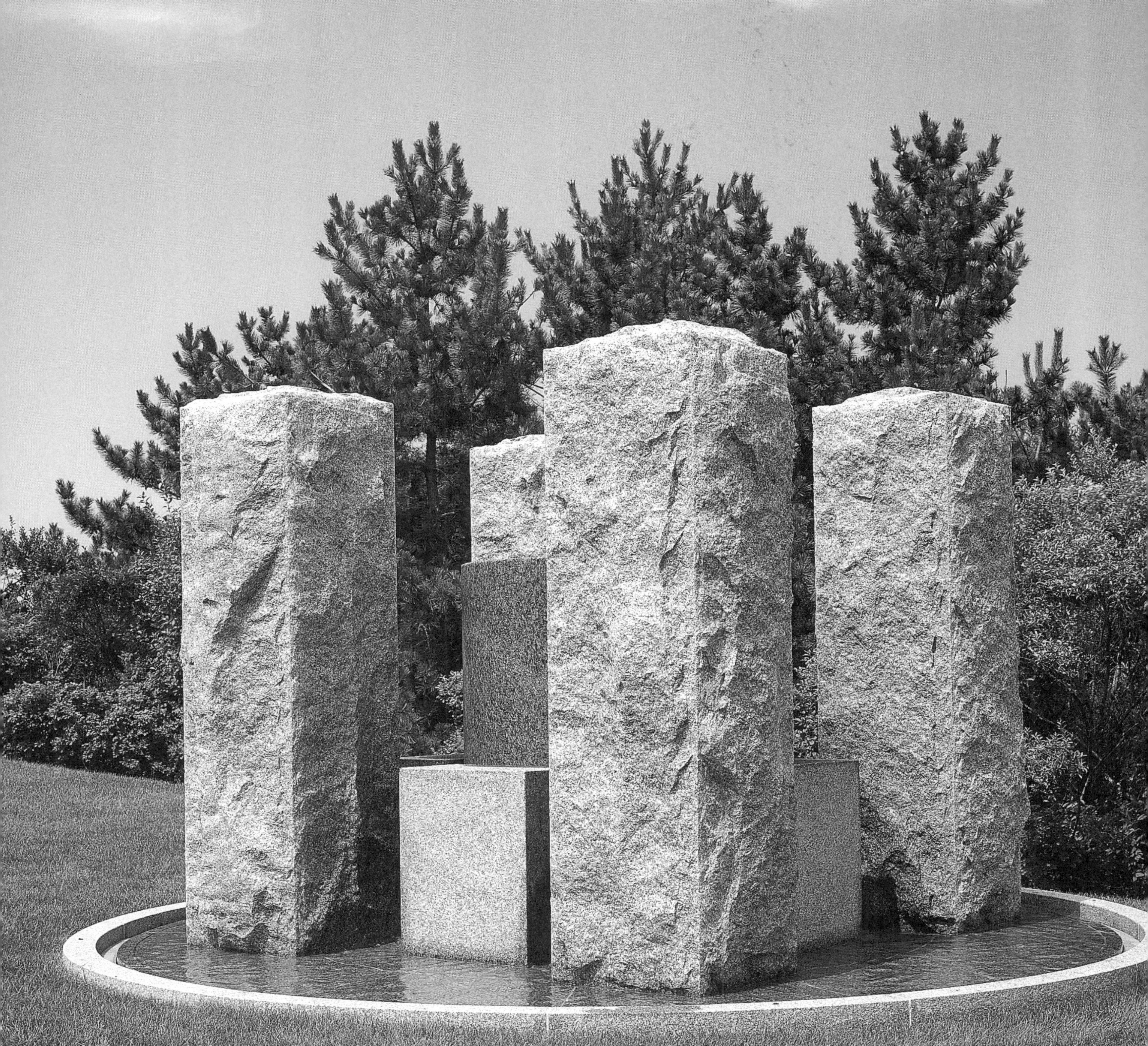

Zimmerman might have made drawings based directly on these photographs, as in her *Equivalent Abstractions* of 1974. But that was a challenge already met and mastered. Rather than mimicking the seamless shading of the photograph, she chose instead to re-enact the overlapping of rhythmic patterns in distinctively graphic terms. She would use exclusively black ink, applied with a brush in regular arcs across the surface of the paper. But no artistic decision is truly simple. Zimmerman soon discovered that conventional "black" inks turned brown when diluted. To get a pure gray, she had to use special inks made with acrylic or graphite pigments. Other technical challenges yielded additional expressive possibilities. Undiluted ink, dragged across the toothy surface of Arches paper, produced a dark line flecked with light where the ink had not penetrated into the paper's crevices. Fabriano, a laid paper with a harder surface, imbued the drawings with a different kind of structure. Diluting the ink not only yielded intermediate shades of gray, but also encouraged it to sink more deeply into the pores of the paper. Wetting the paper ahead of time created new gradients of light and dark, as pigment flowed from the original brushstroke into the damp areas surrounding it. Conversely, a damp sponge or rag could "lift" ink that had already been applied.

Zimmerman executed the first group of drawings using these techniques while still in Vermont. In a vertical sheet from this group (page 33), the first layer of the drawing seems to have been laid in with broad strokes of diluted ink, creating a series of horizontal lines that established a basic "pulse" of light and dark in the background of the picture. Atop this first layer, Zimmerman added a series of darker strokes, curving upwards from left to right. The harder, drier pigment of these strokes contrasts visibly with the softer, more liquid wash of the gray strokes behind them. In another drawing done in Vermont (page 27), Zimmerman retained the structure of darker, denser lines applied over a layer of lighter gray wash. This time it is the darker lines that establish the insistent rhythmic pulse of the drawing, descending from the top in broad dramatic strokes. In contrast, the horizontal gray strokes behind them hold out a promise of serenity.

Tetra, 2000
Detail of pool

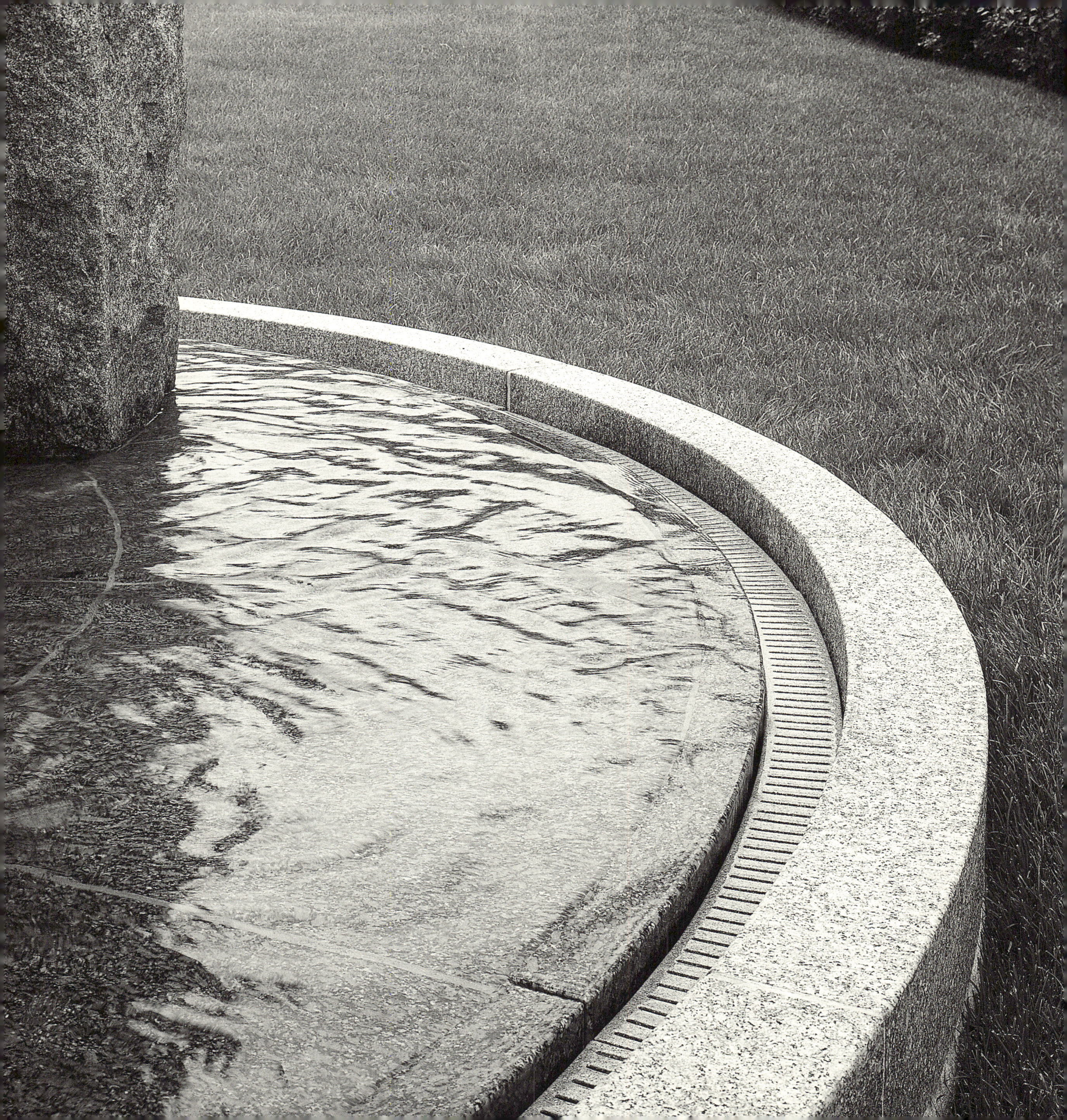

Once she left Vermont, Zimmerman set drawing aside and returned to work on several ongoing sculpture projects. She resumed drawing at Christmas, which she spent in upstate New York. The new drawings were dramatically darker than those in the first series, with an intensified contrast between dark and light. In one vertical sheet (page 35), the upper third of the composition is almost completely filled in by broad bands of black ink. The lower part of the picture is occupied by two series of curved dark bands, one rising from left to right, the other from right to left. The white paper shines brilliantly in the interstices of the overlapping bands, recalling the interlocking patches of sun and shadow in Zimmerman's photographs (page 13). A wet rag seems to have lifted the ink from a horizontal band just below the center, as though a storm were abating somewhere in the distance.

The overlapping curves return in another, horizontal sheet done around Christmas (page 17), but this time the two series are set off by color: the curves descending from upper left seem to have been drawn first, in washes of shifting density, while the curves descending from upper right are darker and drier, slashing aggressively across the surface of the paper, but interrupted by gaps where the brush has lost its grip on the paper. Again, a meteorological comparison is inevitable: the descending strokes evoke lowering clouds (without actually looking like them), and a deluge seems imminent.

The next group of drawings was done in New York, in the first two months of 2001. In the earlier drawings, visual drama had been created largely by the layering of different kinds of strokes, or by the juxtaposition of different kinds of pattern—in other words, by the "interference pattern." In itself, each series of lines or bands was composed of relatively uniform strokes. Zimmerman now began to permit herself broader, bolder strokes, and a greater variety of breadth and orientation within each layer. A vertical sheet (page 31) is bisected by a long dark curve descending from the upper right corner to the lower left, with parallel dark strokes filling the upper left corner and thinner curves filling the lower right corner—a kind of visual ABA pattern. Countering the predominant rhythm, a series of narrow dark lines dangle like filaments of a spider web, descending from left to right. The painterly qualities of upper and lower layers have been reversed: this time it is the lower layers that seem dry and scratchy, and the upper layers that seem smooth and liquid, as though the image had begun to dissolve as it developed.

More recently, in Summer 2001, Zimmerman began to assemble groups of smaller sheets into larger, gridded compositions (page 41). The strokes of cold dark ink descend relentlessly from left to right, forsaking counterpoint in favor of concentration. The motion is continuous across the composition, intensified rather than diminished by the interruptions where one sheet ends and another begins. Inspired, in part, by photographs of a waterfall, these latest drawings seem to capture the urgency of water's incessant flight, moving sideways and downwards across the earth.

At first sight, the black and white gestural vocabulary of Zimmerman's drawings recalls the work of Franz Kline. However, it might be argued that her method has more in common with the impersonal mark-making of Minimalist artists such as Sol LeWitt than with the emotive gestures of Action Painting. The artist's goal here is not to bare her soul but to find an abstract equivalent for the play of patterns she discovered in *Tetra*. The composition of each drawing is predetermined, in effect by Zimmerman's decision to overlap two or three series of wave forms, each one distinguished by its orientation (horizontal or diagonal), its degree of curvature, its breadth, and its density.

Nowhere in this series do individual marks or groups of marks detach themselves from the surrounding framework; there is no dramatic self-assertion of the part against the whole, as there is even in Kline's most abstract work. Rather, the drama of the drawings—sometimes understated, sometimes intense—stems from the behavior of Zimmerman's materials—specifically, from their refusal to be a passive servant of her compositional decisions. The hand cannot always maintain an even pressure. The brush will not release the ink in an even stream; the paper will not receive it evenly. The skipping of a brush, the uneven density of paint, the difference in texture between one layer and another—these evoke the alternation of light and dark on a summer afternoon, the gusts of wind and moments of uncanny stillness, the oppressive humidity and the freshness of air after a storm. This indirect evocation of nature sets Zimmerman's drawings apart from Minimalism, even as their impersonality forbids an identification with Abstract Expressionism.

No doubt the sense of impersonality is itself a kind of façade. Zimmerman may be a willing collaborator in her servants' subtle betrayals. It seems more than a co-incidence, moreover, that the contrasts of texture in her drawings so distinctly echo the contrasts found in her sculptures and installations. The granularity of granite and the fluidity of water reappear in the visual flicker of thick black ink dragged across a "toothed" paper and in the subtle gradations of diluted pigment. Zimmerman's symphonic installations are compressed, here, into concise statements of ink and paper—a chamber music for the eye.

Detail from *Untitled 8*, 2001

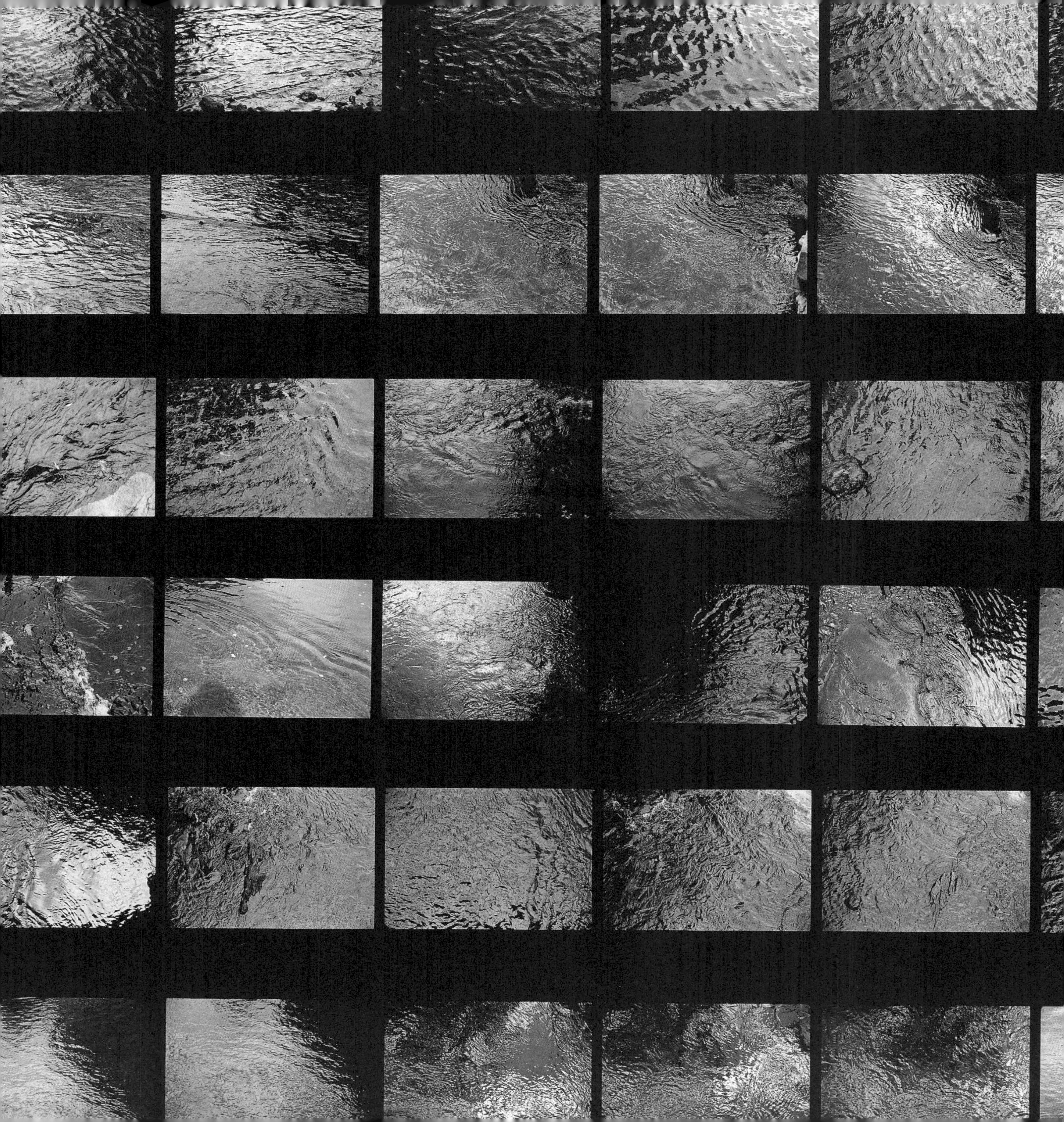

PLATE LIST

PLATE I
Untitled 5, 2000-2001
Sumi ink and graphite wash on paper
22½″ x 30″

PLATE II
Untitled 7, 2001
Sumi ink and graphite wash on paper
22½″ x 30″

PLATE III
Untitled 13, 2001
Sumi ink and watercolour on paper
22½″ x 29½″

PLATE IV
Untitled 11, 2001
Sumi ink on paper
22″ x 29¾″

PLATE V
Untitled 8, 2001
Sumi ink and watercolour on paper
22¼″ x 30″

PLATE VI
Untitled 12, 2000-2001
Ink and graphite wash on paper
30″ x 22″

PLATE VII
Untitled 9, 2001
Sumi ink and watercolour on paper
30″ x 22″

PLATE VIII
Untitled 14, 2000-2001
Sumi ink and watercolour on paper
30″ x 22½″

PLATE IX
Untitled 10, 2000-2001
Ink and graphite wash on paper
30″ x 22½″

PLATE X
Untitled 6, 2000-2001
Sumi ink and graphite wash on paper
30″ x 22¾″

PLATE XI
Untitled 4, 2001
Ink, graphite wash and watercolour on paper
21½″ x 15″

PLATE XII
Untitled 3, 2001
Sumi ink and graphite wash on paper
21¾″ x 15″

PLATE XIII
Riverrun, 2001
Ink and watercolour on paper
42″ x 54″ (9 parts)

Water Study, proof sheet, 2000

Published on the occasion of the exhibition

Elyn Zimmerman: New Drawings
October 11 – November 10, 2001

Gagosian Gallery
980 Madison Avenue
New York, NY 10021
Tel. 212.744.2313
Fax: 212.772.7962
www.gagosian.com

Gagosian Gallery Project Coordinators:
Richie Lasansky, Melissa Lazarov, Jennifer Loh,
Bob Monk and Allison Smith

Publication © Gagosian Gallery 2001

Elyn Zimmerman's Watery Prismatics
© Amy Hempel 2001
New Drawings by Elyn Zimmerman
© Pepe Karmel 2001

ISBN 1-880154-60-9

Photography:
Thomas Powell: pp. 17-41, 61, 63
Colin McRae: p. 45
Tom Van Eynde: p. 49

Design: Bruce Mau Design Inc., Bruce Mau with
Bryan Gee and Amanda Sebris

Typesetting: Archetype, Toronto

Printed in Canada by Bowne, Toronto